CATERPILLAR
DOZERS & TRACTORS

Randy Leffingwell

Lowe & B. Hould
Publishers

This edition published in 2002 by Lowe & B. Hould Publishers, an imprint of Borders, Inc., 515 East Liberty, Ann Arbor, MI 48104. Lowe & B. Hould Publishers is a trademark of Borders Properties, Inc.

First published in 1994 by MBI Publishing Company, Galtier Plaza, Suite 200, 380 Jackson Street, St. Paul, MN 55101-3885 USA

ISBN 0-681-78970-0

On the front cover: 1954 Caterpillar D8. The 13A series was produced from 1953 through 1955 and was Caterpillar's most powerful crawler. At 1200 rpm, Cat rated the engine at 150 drawbar and 185 belt horsepower.

On the frontispiece: Three Best and Caterpillar tractors owned by Doug Veerkamp and his grandfather, George Wagner: 1921 Best Model 30, 1929 Caterpillar Model 60, and 1929 Model Ten.

On the contents page: Logging in the Red River Lumber Company camp. The operator and fireman need to adjust the fuel fire mixture— or just wash their faces. *Jervis Eastman photograph*

On the back cover: 1935 Caterpillar Model RD6. As successors to the Diesel 35, 50, and 75, the RD6, RD7, and RD8 shared common cylinder bore and stroke. But the RD6 used a three-, the RD7 a four-, and the RD8 a six-cylinder engine.

Printed in Hong Kong

Table of Contents

Acknowledgments

This book was a labor of love for many individuals. My thanks first of all go to Edith Heidrick, wife of the late Joe Heidrick, and to Fred Heidrick, Joe's brother, of Woodland, California. Without their great knowledge and extremely generous cooperation and encouragement, much of this book would not exist.

Special thanks to Paul Athorp, Corcoran, California, for his cooperation and explanations of the give-and-take of product development from the customer's perspective; to Albert Dunning, Gridley, California, for explaining the development and economics of butane as a tractor fuel; to Henry Howard, Solvang, California, retired Caterpillar vice-president of sales, for his memory of so many details of so many events; to Wes McKeen, Woodland, California, for his recollections of thirty years of sales and more than a dozen years of Challengers; to Howard Peterson, San Leandro, California, for his recollections of Robert Gilmour LeTourneau and to Emerson Thomas, Westfield, New Jersey, who related the history of odorization of gas, the standards for which he set with his landmark *Bureau of Mines Pamphlet 58* in 1932.

I am extremely grateful and indebted to John Skarstad, Department of Special Collections, University of California, Davis, Library, for his indefatigability. He simply never stopped helping to make this book better and more thorough.

Terry Galloway, Oakland, California generously opened his files and his memory for stories and information on the lives and times of Daniel and C. L. Best. Barry Ward, librarian-archivist at the Library of the Pioneer Museum and Haggin Galleries, Stockton, California, lent his considerable expertise on the subject of the Ben Holt family and company.

Thanks to Robert M. Hanft, Paradise, California, author of *Red River: Paul Bunyan's Own Lumber Company and Its Railroads*, for help in tracking down the earliest Best and Holt steamers.

Special thanks to Anne Fisher, Susanville, California, for her extremely generous access to J. H. Eastman's original collection and for permission to use photographs by the late Jervis H. Eastman, Susanville, California.

My thanks also go to Ed Akin, Placerville, California; Allen Anderson, Ione, Oregon, George Cabral, Ceres, California; Bobby Castro, Kearny, Arizona; Kimberley Christolos, Holt Bros., Stockton, California; Dave Cosyns, Bakersfield, California; Bill Cox, Pomona, California; Buren Craling, Woodland, California; Laurence Darrach, Nicolaus, California; Jack Davis, Nicolaus, California; Mel Eltiste, Playa del Rey, California; Tim Farnham, Woodland, California; Marvin Frey, Salem, Oregon; Harold Gilbert, Knights Landing, California; Alex Giusti, Yuba City, California; Roy E. Hansen Jr., Los Angeles, California; Sam Hatler, Sonora, California; Joe Heidrick Jr., Woodland, California; Tim and Jeri Heidrick, Woodland, California; Don Hunter, Ontario, California; Dave Jopes, Quinn Caterpillar, Fresno, California; Paul Kirsch, St. Paul, Oregon; Joyce Luster, Caterpillar Corporation, Peoria, Illinois; Bill O'Hare, Holt Bros., Stockton, California; Ole Lindberg, Richvale, California; Skip Meyer, Holt Bros., Stockton, California; Bob Older Sr. and Bob Older Jr., Helendale, California; Rick Peterson, Biggs, California; Dick Railing, Wilton, California; Paul Reno, Oakland, California; Lloyd and David Sanders, Durham, California; David and Sylvia Shank, Scottsdale, Arizona; Dave Smith, Woodburn, Oregon; Ed and Bill Stone, Gridley, California; Wayne Swart, Placerville, California; the late Joseph Valine, Sacramento, California; Doug Veerkamp, Placerville, California; Jack Wallace, Woodland, California; Virgil White, Sun Valley, California; Norm Wuytens, Imperial, California; and Ken Yoe, Sacramento, California.

Last, and most of all, I thank Lorry Dunning, historical consultant, Davis, California. He helped this book from its conception to its birth.

Randy Leffingwell
Los Angeles

1914 Holt Model 30
The moon sets over this early Holt gas-engined crawler. It is part of the collection accumulated by the late Joseph Heidrick, Sr. Its serial number, 8180–30008, suggests it may have been the eighth Baby manufactured.

Introduction

Caterpillar History: A Ripping Yarn

Eight hundred horses on their knees is an image that is hard to conjure. As the load brought them down, dragged them to a halt, their cries would hurt the ears. As they struggled to regain their footing—their traction—they would writhe and buck.

Their legs would flail as their steel-shod hooves slashed against the earth and each other. On this cold November morning, vapor would shoot out of their nostrils, like jets, at all angles. It would blast down in white columns and bounce off the ground or ricochet off other horses as their heads strained and twisted. They would radiate steam. And their glistening bodies would shimmer gold translucence in the first red-orange sunlight. The reins of this massive 800-horse team would take more than a mile of leather lacework to feed control back to one individual perched high above the herd.

Gouging into a California high desert pasture takes a ripper. This November morning, it's a pointed spike taller than a man that tapers to something like a ball-point pen. The ground here steams. It's own heat leaks out from the fresh wound ripped into it. On this November morning near the middle of the final decade of the Twentieth Century, such a vision is possible—such a feat is accomplished—because all those horses have been encapsulated into one Caterpillar Model D11N crawler. With its 22ft-wide blade, it stretches nearly 30ft in length. What would have taken one million pounds of animals spread over nearly two-thirds of an acre is now compressed into 242,000lb in just 600sq-ft.

But Jurassic-era hard pan compressed 7ft below the pastoral surface does not yield without a fight.

A rule of thumb recommends one flywheel horsepower per 90–100lb of down pressure, with 2–3lb of tractor weight per pound of ripper tooth pressure to guarantee adequate traction against the ground's resistance.

Tractor operator Sam Hatler lightly grasps two knobs near his left forearm. Shaped like airplane throttles, these levers serve the track clutches and brakes. There is no equivalent on a horse-drawn rig beyond powerful arms and a strong voice hollering "gee" or "haw".

Hatler delicately feathers his controls. His right toe teases the decelerator. His right hand plays a joystick ripper control like an adept video-game competitor. Hatler is 30 years old, strong, hefty, agile. He sits in a weight adjustable seat and watches a wide rearview mirror over his head. Below him, the spike waggles; behind him is the arrow-straight scar he has made in the earth.

Beneath him, the mass of Caterpillar squirms and thunders. The density of the earth is humbling. The crawler's broad, steel tracks rise behind Hatler's cab and climb upward and then forward across the drive gear. They plunge down toward the blade and plummet again to the ground, only to reemerge seconds later. The tracks are nearly clean. The hard ground has stopped the tractor—seized the spike—scouring the tracks as they wipe across its surface.

Now the engine holds the note of a tenor with good control. Its voice does not vary. Gears moan their complaint as Hatler gets the horses moving again. Inches, then feet at a time.

One pass done east-to-west across this ninety-acre field takes 30 minutes. There are now only 209 more passes to go: 104 1/2 hours of east to west and back, and then 105 hours north to south and back.

The ripper is opening up clay. Hatler's customer intends to plant Eucalyptus trees in this stuff. Cutting the north boundary, Hatler explains that the Eucalyptus will deflect the wind from fragile apple trees to be planted in the rest of this orchard. In the old days, Hatler says, men drilled holes and planted dynamite to break up this soil. The explosions opened it enough so that water would flow and tree roots could grow.

Visualizing all of Hatler's ninety acres lifted 10ft in the air is as confounding as knowing that one square foot of this land has humbled the D11.

Hatler must rip all these ninety acres to open the rest of his client's future orchard. He says it will take a week-and-a-half of 14 hour days. He rips an acre and a fifth each hour, an inch and a foot at a time. Long days he accepts. He knows

1993 Caterpillar D11N

Ground force is 22psi, the same as a 200lb man standing on tiptoes. Yet each 28in track set plus its track roller frame—per side—weighed 33,430lb, a few pounds shy of two fully equipped 1917 Holt Model 75s.

1993 Caterpillar D11N

Right, scale is deceptive. The D11N is nearly 15ft tall and the ripper is buried 7ft deep in northern California clay. At 1mph, the 770hp Caterpillar exerts more than 185,000lb of ripper pull.

1993 Caterpillar D11N

Opposite page, the ground steams, its heat erupting from the gash. The hard-packed clay resists nearly 30 tons of downforce and stops the crawler, spinning the tracks, allowing no forward movement.

they're necessary because the machine is so costly. Long days give customers, owners and operators their money's worth.

A new D11N sells for nearly $1,000,000. That's about $1,250 for each horsepower. Hatler's customer doesn't know that a mature Percheron or Belgian draft horse can cost as much as $5,000 a head, and he wouldn't understand that those horses couldn't possibly do an acre per hour.

And Hatler's customer wouldn't want to think about what happens if almost 800 horses go to their knees. Because the nearly 800hp machine he has hired won't.

Chapter 1

Best of the West

Daniel Best Moves West and Sets Up Shop ✦ *Birth of C. L. Best* ✦
Early American Steam Traction Engines ✦ *Daniel Best Agricultural Works*
Founded in 1886 ✦ *Best's First Patents* ✦ *D. L. Remington's "Rough and Ready"*
Steamer ✦ *The Best Steam Traction Engine* ✦ *"Monarchs of the Field"*

Daniel Best

1904 Best Steamer

Opposite page, it measured 22ft long.

Its rear drive wheels measured 8ft in

diameter and it offered its operators

6ft-6in of stand-up headroom. Daniel

Best's 175th steamer was owned by the

late Joseph Heidrick, Sr, and is one of

336 produced.

Everything was supposed to be easier once they got to the West. Daniel Best's brother Samuel Best, older by a decade and living in Oregon for seven years, had written back to the family from Portland. Life in the West was good, he'd said in 1859. There was work. There were opportunities.

Ten years before Samuel lured his younger brother to go west, gold had been discovered in California, at Sutter's Mill, about thirty miles east of Sacramento. More than 300,000 men, women, and children headed west during the following dozen years. They hungered for the same opportunities that Samuel and countless other transplants, emigrants, and newspapers had written about.

Daniel Best was born in Ohio on March 28, 1838, the ninth child of sixteen from his father John's two marriages. When Daniel was six, his family moved to Missouri, where his father established a sawmill. When Daniel was nine, John Best and family moved again, to Vincennes, Iowa, twelve miles from Keokuk. According to Terry Galloway, great-grandson and biographer of Daniel Best, the sawmill was profitable enough that the Bests eventually acquired and farmed more than 400 acres, raising corn and cattle. Life was good for the Bests and good enough for Daniel— that is, until Samuel's letters came home to Iowa. The legends from Samuel's pen enticed Daniel to go west as well. In 1859, he signed onto a wagon train as a guard and sharpshooter.

No farther from home than Nebraska, the twenty-one-year-old farmer had already survived stampedes, ambushes, perilous escapes, and dwindling supplies. Once across Wyoming and into Idaho, the thirty wagons of 100 travelers split into three groups. Best lead a small pack across the tip of Oregon toward Washington.

Settling in Steptoville (now called Walla Walla), Best found jobs at what he knew. With a companion, he first worked at a lumber mill and then later established his own mill in town. Business ambitions led him to Portland, where he again worked for a lumber mill. His father died in

1861 and his brothers Henry (six years older) and Zachariah (a year younger than Daniel) moved to California. Henry headed to Yuba City, while Zach settled in Sutter County. (Over the next thirty years, another six of Daniel's brothers and sisters would move to Yuba or Sutter counties in the center of California.) When Daniel was twenty-four, he and a partner invested in a gold mine in the Powder River Valley in southern Washington. After some successful strikes, Best lost it all: Floating down the Snake River, his raft spilled him and his treasure into the rapids. He barely escaped with his life.

Between 1862 and 1869, Daniel moved back and forth between mining and lumbering, making and losing fortunes with regularity in each trade. It was during one of the lumbering episodes in late 1868 near Olympia, Washington, that he lost three fingers on his left hand in a saw mill accident. A year later, he moved back south to Marysville, near Yuba City—about forty miles north of Sacramento— and began working with his brother Henry on his ranch.

After Henry's grain harvest, Daniel learned that they and their neighbors had to have their grain cleaned before it could be sold. To do so, they had to haul their grain into Marysville and pay $3 per ton for the job. Daniel began thinking about how to clean the grain at the farm—how to transport the cleaner to the grain rather than haul the grain into town.

During the winter, Daniel worked with Henry and Zach developing a transportable cleaner. For the 1870 harvest season, the three brothers each operated one of Daniel's new machines. The brothers and their machines were efficient—capable of between thirty and sixty tons per day— and for his competent machine, Best was awarded a patent in April 1871. Biographer Galloway learned that later that year, Best took on a fifty-fifty partner, L. D. Brown of Marysville, to expand production. Brown fed the demand for their cleaner by opening a manufacturing plant. That same year, their "Best and Brown's Unrivaled Seed Separator" won a first-place prize at the California State Fair.

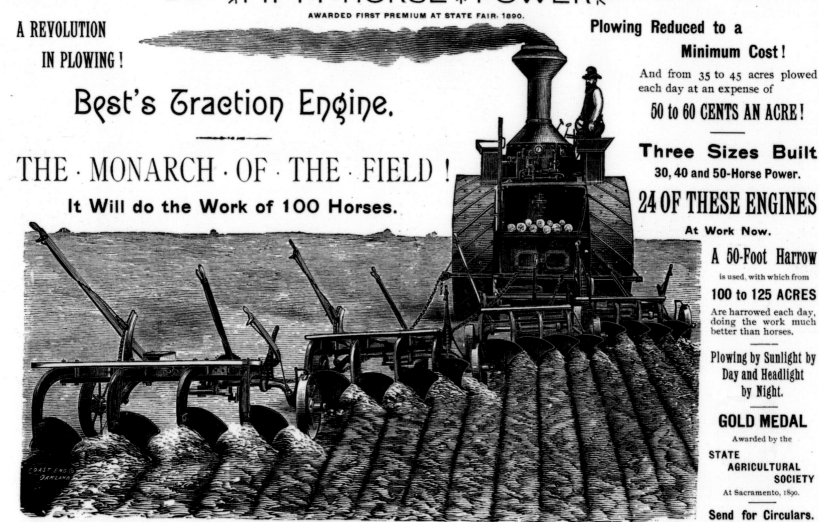

DANIEL · BEST'S · STEAM · PLOW.

⇥ FIFTY-HORSE ⁜ POWER ⇤

AWARDED FIRST PREMIUM AT STATE FAIR, 1890.

A REVOLUTION IN PLOWING !

Best's Traction Engine.

THE · MONARCH · OF · THE · FIELD !

It Will do the Work of 100 Horses.

Plowing Reduced to a Minimum Cost !

And from 35 to 45 acres plowed each day at an expense of **50 to 60 CENTS AN ACRE !**

Three Sizes Built
30, 40 and 50-Horse Power.

24 OF THESE ENGINES
At Work Now.

A 50-Foot Harrow
is used, with which from **100 to 125 ACRES**
Are harrowed each day, doing the work much better than horses.

Plowing by Sunlight by Day and Headlight by Night.

GOLD MEDAL
Awarded by the **STATE AGRICULTURAL SOCIETY**
At Sacramento, 1890.

Send for Circulars.

As seen at work in Fresno County pulling **SIXTEEN 10-INCH PLOWS** at the speed of 3 miles per hour, cutting over 13 feet

---

Circa 1900 Best 50hp Steam Plow

Daniel Best advertisement for

"The Monarch of the field!"

Higgins collection

The Bests charged the same fee—$3 per ton—for on-site cleaning and separating as the operators in town had done. But their service allowed farmers to keep their grain on their own farms, saving them the additional storage fees that the town cleaners charged. Running at sixty and sometimes seventy tons per day, their operation was lucrative.

Daniel Best was an inveterate tinkerer, and was awarded a second patent for his seed coating machine. Brown continued manufacturing the separators and Best, married in 1872, returned to gold mining in 1874. Again, a boom preceded a bust. But even as his mine failed, he received his

third patent in May 1877, for an improvement on an existing clothes washing machine.

On April 21, 1878, while Daniel was working as a lumber mill manager in Albany, Oregon, his wife gave birth to their third child, a son, Clarence Leo Best. That summer, it became a requirement of Oregon farmers that their grain be cleaned before sale or transport, just as California had mandated. Best quickly returned to the separator business, and with Nathaniel Slate, a local partner in Albany, he received advanced orders for forty of his machines.

A year later, Best opened a branch in Oakland, commuting frequently from his home in Oregon. Business flourished because Oakland was a primary brokers' market and a shipping port for grain and wheat. Even working his plant to its capacity, demand for Best's machines exceeded his ability to produce.

According to Galloway, Daniel Best had pondered for some time the idea of incorporating various functions into one machine. Farmers had told him of their desire to combine into one process harvesting, cleaning, and even bagging. He knew such machines existed; they had been available in Iowa since the 1830s. The harvesters for eastern farms were too small to be adapted, however, so with Slate, he manufactured his first combination harvester/separator with headers offering 20ft to 40ft cuts. His advertising was specific: "These machines are especially adapted to large farms, and are only made on order are guaranteed to work as well as the smaller size and [in] any place where you can work a common header."

Best also made smaller machines with 14ft headers. But the vast acreages of some California farmers challenged him. The large machines that Best built to meet their needs sometimes went beyond the abilities of even the largest horse teams to manage. For harvesters with headers as large as 40ft, he needed more horsepower.

Restless and filled with energy, Best and his family moved over to Klickitat, Washington. Lumbering, milling, mining, and farming continued to occupy his time and interests.

Starting the 110hp Best Oil-Fired Steam Traction Engine

1. Walk around the machine, inspecting it for lose bolts or other fittings. Tighten, repair, or replace any as necessary.
2. Remove the stack cover.
3. Check the water levels in the water tank and boiler. Check the trycocks to confirm the water glass reading.
4. Place wood carefully into the firebox so that the firebrick lining is not damaged. Light a fire.
5. While the wood is burning and steam pressure is building, fill all the oil cups and mechanical and hydrostatic lubricators. Turn the grease cup caps down and add grease if needed to properly lubricate all parts. Oil all oil holes in moving machinery.
6. When steam pressure reaches 70–80psi, check the steam-operated injectors to make certain that water can be supplied to the boiler. Clean supply-side strainers if necessary.
7. When steam pressure reaches 80–100psi, turn steam on to atomizer while the oil burner is out of the firebox and pointed away from the machine. This lets water and condensed steam blow into the atmosphere and does not interfere with fire. After the lines are clean and the burner is heated, place the burner through an aperture in firebox door.
8. Turn on the steam to the atomizer.
9. Turn on the oil through the firing valve, and turn on the draft when oil starts burning. Adjust atomizer steam if necessary.
10. Watch the stack for proper smoke color. If the smoke is too black, decrease the amount of oil. If the smoke is blue, increase the amount of oil. The stack should show a slight haze when the fire is burning properly.
11. Monitor the draft, atomizer, and oil as steam pressure rises. Adjust accordingly.
12. Turn the steam on to hydrostatic lubricator.
13. Make certain all drains are open to valve chests and cylinders. Make certain all valve chests and cylinder drains are open.
14. Make certain all drains are open on the steering engine (if the engine is equipped with steam-powered steering assist).
15. When boiler pressure reaches maximum working pressure (depending on the engine), make certain that the safety valve works properly by watching the steam gauge and making certain that the valve opens at the proper pressure and closes again at the proper pressure.
16. Make certain that the engine is disengaged from the driveshaft. Turn the hydrostatic lubricator valves on to the engine.
17. Open the throttle slightly so that a small amount of steam is supplied to the engine. The engine will idle slowly and will warm up slowly and evenly.
18. Once the engine is warmed up, shut the throttle to stop it. Engage the drive gear.
19. Be certain that the area around the tractor is clear of obstructions and that the stack will clear all overhanging trees or structures. Open the throttle gently and move the tractor forward and backward. Turn left and right to check the operation of the steering engine.
20. Shut all drains. The tractor is ready to work.

Caution: Allow 1 1/2 hours for starting procedure.

Best 110hp Steamer and

Best Balance-Beam Harvester

Right, harvesting wheat with Best 110hp
steamer and Best balance-beam harvester
required a handful of workers. The
engine operator and firemen were joined
by the harvester crew.

Higgins collection

C. L. Best and 110hp Best Steamer

Below, C. L. Best (in the passenger seat)
watches his oil-fired 110hp steamer
harvesting with a Best 40ft header
combined steam harvester in Los Angeles
sometime around 1906. A 55gal oil
drum sits above the front tiller wheel.

Higgins collection

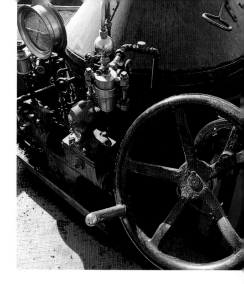

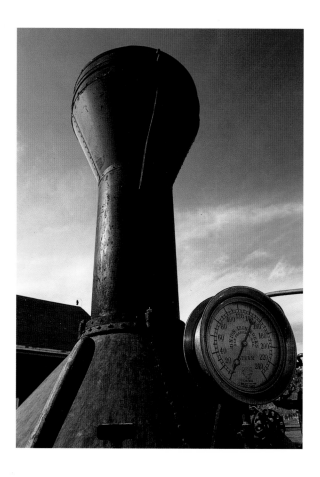

In Oakland, his manufacturing business continued at its fast pace. More patents followed in 1883 and 1884 as he continually improved his cleaners and combined harvester/separators. There was no longer enough room in his small yard to store the machines ready for delivery, forcing him to leave them on Oakland's side streets surrounding his factory. When the Oakland police complained about this, he knew it was time to expand and sensed it was time to move.

Galloway reported that Best sold some of his interests in Oregon and Washington, and then took $15,000 and returned to the Oakland area to look at San Leandro, a city he had admired on earlier visits. In late October 1886, he spent $12,000 and purchased Jacob Price's business and shops, The San Leandro Plow Company. The newly founded Daniel Best Agricultural Works consolidated all the machinery and production from Albany and Oakland. According to Galloway, in March 1887, Best applied for patents on both a combined header and thresher and on a "fan blast" governor that blew the grain against the drums at a uniform pressure and regulated the internal machinery of the combine without regard to the ground speed that the horses provided.

Within another three years, farmers in California, Oregon, and Washington put 150 Best combined harvesters to work. His blast fan governor was a strong first step toward quality control in grain harvesting and cleaning in a single machine.

When gold was discovered forty years before, one of those who had seen the opportunities was a Missouri medical doctor named Hugh Glenn. But Dr. Glenn arrived in

1904 Best Steamer

Above, recent research indicates that Best manufactured 336 of the giant 110hp steamers. In addition, it produced 112 of the 75hp versions and between 40–50 of the 50hp engines. The giants sold new for around $5,500.

1904 Best Steamer

Upper left, when boiler pressure reaches 80–100psi, the engine is ready for work. Its 940gal water tank capacity gave the steamer a working range of about 7.5 miles, evaporating 125gal per mile. But the 22,000lb engines could tow 72,000lb up a 12 percent grade.

1904 Best Steamer

Left, this example, Best's 185th, was restored by and is owned by the City of Oakland Museum. It can be seen at the Ardenwood Historical Farm, Fremont, California. Volunteer members fire the wood-burner on occasional weekends.

1904 Best Steamer

Right, Daniel Best produced steam traction engines in 50hp, 75hp, and 110hp versions; this is a 110. The tall, slender, rear drive wheels suggest that this model was used for logging or freighting rather than agriculture.

1904 Best Steamer

Below, overall this giant steamer is 28ft long. A 6ft tall operator stands nearly 16ft above the ground. The view toward the front tiller wheel is obscured by the 940gal water tank. The arrow indicates the direction of the front wheel.

California untempted by pick, pan, or shovel. Knowing that those who went after the elusive metal would need their equipment—if not their gold—hauled, he started a freight business. He purchased equipment locally, buying first wheels and spokes for repairs and then entire wagons. His business was very successful. He sold it and, still disinterested in mining, looked into another kind of California gold: land on which to raise wheat.

In 1867, Dr. Glenn acquired a 7,000-acre Spanish land grant ranch. He reaped another profit and bought more land. By 1876, he owned 45,000 acres, and in a few years, his fields were producing one million bushels of grain. Stories circulated in San Francisco newspapers that Dr. Glenn's fields ran eighteen miles in uninterrupted length along the Sacramento River. His crews began at sunrise and plowed or harvested in a straight line, stopped for lunch, and then continued along the same line until nightfall. Before bedding down, they turned all their equipment around so that the next morning they would be ready to head back to the opposite end. They set a record for a single day's harvest on July 26, 1879, an event that was chronicled in the *Willow Journal*, the newspaper from the town nearest to Glenn's ranch, and later quoted in Stewart Holbrook's

1955 book, *Machines of Plenty*: "At sunset, the official count of the sacks was made, the total being 6,183 bushels of wheat cut, threshed, and garnered from sun to sun."

This was accomplished with J. I. Case machinery from Racine, Wisconsin, that had been shipped all the way around the Horn. But it was this scale of farming that inspired Daniel Best. Running the six combines on the Glenn ranch had required 150 horses. Setting the harvest record called for nearly 1,000 workers. Best believed that another method must exist that would save manpower and horsepower.

In 1869, Philander Standish and Riley Doan had built a 12hp steam traction engine, the Mayflower steam rotary plow, in Pacheco, California. Self-propelled steam traction engines manufactured by Merritt & Kellog of Michigan had appeared in the Midwest as early as 1873. Portables—engines mounted on wheels and driven by horses—first appeared in Philadelphia in 1849. However, these were wood or coal burners; straw burners suited to the treeless western prairies came later, and oil-fired burners appeared later still. In 1886, George Berry of Visalia (midway between Sacra-

Best 110hp Steamer

Those extension rims are nearly 12ft on each side on this Best 110hp. Front tank ahead of boiler is oil reservoir for firing the boiler. Higgins collection

mento and Los Angeles) operated the first steam-powered combine; Berry's steamer burned straw for fuel.

Price already knew about these machines—and about others who were advancing the technology. By 1887, the name Marquis De Lafayette Remington—and his work with steam—had come to Price's attention. Since selling his San Leandro Plow Company plant to Best, Price had become a friend. According to biographer Terry Galloway, Price had assembled a steam traction engine in his former shop where Best now built his combines. Price's engine was

1904 Best Steamer

Left, above the steamer's 5ft-6in tall front wheel, steam bleeds off the power steering engine. In neutral, the 52in flywheel sits idle and the well-adjusted oil burner allows a clean exhaust from the tall stack.

1904 Best Steamer

Opposite page far left, the top of its canopy, 17ft-6in above the ground, dwarfs steam engineer Ken Yoe. Here, Yoe turns on the water injector. This complex plumbing is necessary to to fuel this oil-fired steam traction engine.

1904 Best Steamer

Opposite page upper right, there is nothing delicate here. Boiler steam feeds two 9.00x9.00in cylinders. The crankshaft drives gears to power the rear drive wheels.

1904 Best Steamer

Opposite page lower right, the 15in steering wheel maneuvers the 11 ton engine easily. Separate lines from the main steam boiler feed an auxiliary steam engine that provides power steering.

configured as a road roller as Price had been contracted to crush rock for San Jose's streets. With his assembly complete, he began tests in mid-October 1887. As a rock crusher, his machine was a failure, but in Best's eyes it had possibilities as a traction engine.

Remington, a blacksmith, had produced his first steam traction engine out of his foundry and machine shops in Woodburn, Oregon, in 1885. It had performed well in agriculture and logging, and was patented in January 1888. Two months later in early spring, knowing of the name and reputation of Best's combined harvesters, Remington and his second traction engine took the Oregonian Railroad south to San Leandro. Demonstrations began right in front of Daniel Best's shops.

The crowds were no more impressed than Best himself. He bought the rights to manufacture Remington's 30hp "Rough and Ready"; Best would sell it everywhere on the West Coast outside of Remington's home state. Through the rest of the year, Best worked to incorporate Remington's steam traction engine into his own product. Galloway described the result: "This was a spectacular new invention which had two parts, the traction engine and the combined harvester. The engine pulled the combine faster and over rougher terrain than teams could and it supplied steam to

power an auxiliary engine on the harvester. The combine had a conveyor to carry [threshed] straw to a receptacle close to the boiler, so the combine cut its own fuel as it went along!"

By the end of 1888, Best had applied for a patent on this combination, which was awarded to him in September 1889. Two months after the application was filed, Best sold his first steam traction engine for $4,500 to John Butler, who farmed near Red Bluff.

Best had modified Remington's design. He replaced Remington's wrought-iron frame with steel. He enlarged the water tank and boiler, resulting in nearly 50 more horsepower, and he increased ground clearance by more than 2ft to improve maneuverability.

Embittered over his own failure and the success of Remington and Best, Price left town, still holding on to the vision of 50, 100, and even 150hp tractors working vast spreads of wheat. According to Holbrook, "One day in the late 1880s, there came into the [J. I.] Case offices a man who said he came from San Leandro, California, an ungrateful town, he went on, and inhospitable to inventors. His name was Jacob Price, he told the Case people. He had already built a steam road-roller and he was now ready to build a steam rig that would pull any number of plows, go uphill and down, and stop at nothing.

Best 110hp Steamer

Logging at the Red River Lumber company with Best 110hp traction engines. Jervis Eastman photograph

"For many years, the notion prevailed that combines could be used effectively only in a few regions where dry weather came with the harvest season, where the straw stood erect for many days after the grain ripened, and where there were no winds or rains to cause lodging or tangling. It is understandable that such enormous machines were confined mostly to the immense wheat ranches of the Far West."

But once farmers like the Glenns and Butlers began operating the large machines, they recognized the savings and profits that equipment of this scale presented to them. With a steamer and a combined harvester, three men could do what it had taken twenty to accomplish with a binder and threshing machine. Local newspapers reported that what had cost farmers and land owners $3 to $4 per acre to harvest now cost $1 to $1.50 with the arrival of combines and steam. When Midwestern manufacturers began producing smaller machines, Midwest farmers wasted little time in using them.

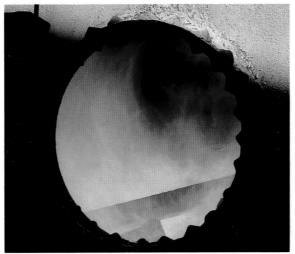

1904 Best Steamer

Above six four-bottom 16in plow gangs trail off behind the Best steamer. This kind of performance was loafing. Best's 110hp steamers have pulled thirty-six 7in plows through clay or adobe over as much as 12 acres an hour.

1904 Best Steamer

Left, in the belly of the beast the fire is started with kindling and fireplace logs.

1904 Best Steamer

Put in scale, a 6ft tall man stands dwarfed by 8ft tall, 5ft wide drive wheels on this agricultural steamer. Best's longer steamers used for freighting were known for dragging more than three times their weight up nearly 1:6 grades.

110hp Bests and Best Steam Harvesters
Left, in the harvest camp, a couple visitors pose for a photograph with 110hp Bests and Best steam harvesters. Higgins collection

Best & Brown Combined Harvester
Below, a Combined Harvester works the rolling hills behind a twenty-six-horse team. Higgins collection

Chapter 2

Holt Conquers the Hills

Charles Henry Holt Goes West ✦ *Stockton Wheel Company Founded in 1883* ✦ *Holt Manufacturing Company Founded* ✦ *The Holt Bros. Improved Link Belt Combined Harvester* ✦ *"Old Betsy"* ✦ *Holt Versus Best* ✦ *Early Tracklayers* ✦ *The First "Caterpillar"*

In 1865, six years after Daniel Best fought his way to Oregon, Charles Henry Holt disembarked from a ship in San Francisco. Born in 1843 in Loudon, near Concord, New Hampshire, Charles was schooled and trained in accounting in Boston. In 1864, he moved to New York and, working as an accountant for a shipping company, he listened to tales sea captains told of life in California. A year later, promised a job in San Francisco, the twenty-two-year-old sailed around the tip of South America.

The job in San Francisco never materialized, but within a year, Charles found a teaching job—accounting, presumably—in Hydesville, about 200 miles north of San Francisco. To supplement his income and build savings, he kept books for a local merchant after school. Within two years, he had accumulated $700 and—ambitions now financed—he thought again about San Francisco.

The Holt family business in Concord was lumber. Charles' father William was a lumber dealer who specialized in the hardwoods used in manufacturing wagons. Charles and his brothers, Frank, William Jr., and Benjamin, had all worked in the family business. Given the development and growth in the West, Charles knew there was a need for hardwoods for freight wagons and stage coaches. In 1869, he returned to San Francisco and established C. H. Holt & Company. He bought wood from his father and sold it in San Francisco to wagon and boat makers. Younger brother Frank soon joined him, establishing a branch of the family's lumber business in Concord to produce wagon wheels and the pieces for making them. Meanwhile, older brother William withdrew from the family businesses, selling his interest to his brothers.

The youngest boy, Benjamin, named after his grandfather, was born in Loudon, New Hampshire, on New Years day, 1849. Benjamin, as thoroughly educated as his older brothers, joined his father's firm when he was 20.

Brother Charles' customers had begun to experience wheel failures. California lacked the humidity of New England, and the wheels manufactured in Concord were not seasoned properly to survive the long, hot, dry summers. Charles began bringing wood to San Francisco for seasoning and manufacture. When even this failed to remedy the problems, the Holt brothers looked inland to Stockton for a manufacturing site.

Stockton was a well-regarded city in the 1870s. It was a center of commerce close to the farming interests of the San Joaquin Valley, and it served as a manufacturing center for the unique products that miners needed in the mountains far to the east of the city. In addition, the San Joaquin River provided direct shipping access to San Francisco ninety miles west. In 1883, the Holt brothers founded Stockton Wheel Company. Thirty-four-year-old Benjamin was brought out from Concord to take charge. When Frank died in 1886, Charles and Benjamin bought his interest in Stockton Wheel from his widow and sold her their portions of the Concord business. California now belonged to Charles and Benjamin.

In 1935, Charles Parker Holt, executive vice-president of Caterpillar and a son of Charles Holt, prepared a draft of "Early Developments of the Holt Manufacturing Company." Directed to G. B. Walker, Caterpillar's advertising manager, for corporate use, this manuscript filled in many blanks in the family's history.

The brothers had become aware of the increasing trade in harvesting machinery. Combined harvesters had been around for more than two decades in California—J. I. Case company records tell of shipping threshers around the Horn to California in 1860—and much longer back east. But most of the competition relied on gears, pinions, shafts, and countershafts to transmit the power from one segment of the machine to another. These required constant attention. Even when properly cleaned and lubricated, the gears wore quickly and their clatter had been known to cause horse runaways, frequently with disastrous results. Operators were hurt or killed, horses were injured and had to be put down. Newspapers regularly reported harvesters destroyed from rollovers and crashes.

Ben Holt

1915 Caterpillar School Badge

Opposite page, Holt and Best operated schools for their new customers and refresher programs for existing owners as well, done in conjunction with a local sales office. Often these were sales opportunities to show off new products.

Charles Holt's business skills matched Benjamin's abilities and interest in mechanical devices. From their father's lumber and milling operation, Benjamin knew the capabilities of belt-driven pulleys. But under load, belts slipped. Sprocket-driven link belts would handle much more power. These were essentially a chain with interchangeable links that could be reassembled or replaced if one broke. It was a short leap to imagine a link belt much more quietly and efficiently connecting all the functions of a combine. The brothers acquired the licenses to a few patents and bought several others outright. In 1886, they began to produce The Holt Bros. Improved Link Belt Combined Harvester. According to Charles Parker Holt, the word "improved" referred to features that Benjamin and Charles "built into their harvesters, such as a single front wheel with a turntable, a hinged header, and the method of balancing the header by beams and weights so that it could be easily raised and lowered."

They claimed that their "quiet" combine had caused no runaways and advertised several improvements, among them the use of "V" belts, tapered leather belts, to connect the threshing cylinder shaft to its drive, and "a cleaner at the top and on the main wheel side of the harvester to clean the grain as it came from the separator."

In the late 1880s, farmers and land developers devoted a great deal of energy and money to reclaiming lands in the delta of the San Joaquin and Sacramento Rivers south of Stockton. This land—some 500,000 acres—was fertile and quite flat, but it was also soft. The pliant soil was hard going for horses, even those wearing oversized steel shoes that literally scarred the fields, and it took a toll on machinery. Both the Holt harvesters with headers up to 32ft per cut and Best's machines with cuts of 40ft offered the greatest economy and efficiency in harvesting these areas. (These harvesters required at least two dozen head, sometimes and as many as four dozen, and the harvesters bogged down, sinking to their axles or beyond.)

Conditions facing Western farmers were more diverse than those that farmers in the Midwest and East had to accommodate. Geography placed obstacles—and opportunities—in their paths. In California, Oregon, and Washington, farmers not only looked longingly at riverside lowlands, they also knew that the rolling foothills offered soil nearly as appealing as the flat valley floors. But negotiating the hills was as great a challenge as it was to stay afloat in the peat.

While Benjamin Holt mused over a solution to farming the soft delta bottom lands, the hills around Stockton brought about a significant and successful Holt invention in 1890. Early combines were narrow, top-heavy affairs mounted on narrow-gauge wooden wheels that sometimes toppled over if the long wheat-cutting headers got too far off balance. Even before tipping, the grain would not travel properly inside a tilted harvester. Holt developed a "side-hill" harvester that featured adjustable wheel height and header angle so that the harvester box was always vertical regardless of the angle of the hill. Word of this development spread through the West, and Holt shipped side-hill harvesters throughout California and to Oregon and Washington. Suddenly, hundreds of thousands of acres could be planted and harvested economically.

At about this same time, Holt Manufacturing introduced the steam traction engine that Benjamin invented, nicknamed "Old Betsy." Following through with his belief in chain drive, Holt avoided gears in his steamer. Friction arms operated the flywheels. The engine was reversible, but there was neither a transmission nor differential. "Betsy" weighed a trim 48,000lb but reportedly could pull thirty plow bottoms and plant forty acres a day. Best—and Remington before him—had mounted the 4ft-diameter boiler upright, fitted between the two 8ft-tall drive wheels attached to a heavy iron frame. With a rated pressure of 150psi, Best had claimed 60hp and drove two 9x9in cylinders. Best's engine weighed 22,000lb.

Holt laid the boiler on its side, unlike the competition and more like that used in railroad locomotives. He used only a single 10.25x12in cylinder. At 150psi boiler pressure, Holt claimed 70hp. However, the chief distinction between "Old Betsy" and all the others was that Holt incorporated steering clutches. This mechanism disengaged power to one driving wheel or the other to provide sharper turning ability. Holt was awarded a patent for this idea in 1893.

A year earlier, the name of the company was changed from The Stockton Wheel Company to The Holt Manufacturing Company, to better reflect the broader nature of the company's expanding business. Benjamin's inventiveness and Charles' business acumen brought them not only more orders for both steamers and combines, it made them aware of improvements and developments from other producers. And on the evidence of their own successful patents, their business successes impressed upon them the advantage of acquiring for themselves the ownership of other inventors' ideas.

In 1895, Benjamin and Charles acquired Matteson & Williamson Manufacturing Co., a Stockton maker of the Harvest "Prince" combined harvester. By 1900, the Holt brothers had produced 1,072 combines, more than all their competition together. Still ambitious, they acquired Houser & Haines, another harvester maker in Stockton, the next year.

Holt had become Best's primary competitor. They built similar machines, although Holt concentrated more on combined harvesters, whereas Best specialized in traction engines. Even though Best had built his steam combine first, in the spring of 1889, Holt had quickly followed and then took a substantial production lead. By 1912, Best had built 1,351 steam combines—but Holt had built 8,000.

Best and Holt relied on their strong dealer networks to respond quickly to grain growers' needs. Their steam traction engines were also used in Oregon and Washington to haul lumber from the forests to the railhead. And both manufacturers saw increasing use in "freighting"—towing large wagons loaded with supplies and material—and in construction. Benjamin Holt even established his own freight company.

The primary use for their steamers remained the planting and harvesting of grain. Working on the peat of the low-

lands between Stockton and Sacramento, 6ft-wide extension rims were fitted—often in multiples—to the standard wheels to keep these eleven- and twenty-two-ton heavyweights from sinking into the soft, watery soil. Tractor widths of 46ft were marvels to behold but were not uncommon.

This much power produced stunning performances. Newspapers published stories of the Best machines, called the "Monarchs of the Field," cutting swaths 48ft wide and clearing 100 acres a day. Other reports told of Holts cut-

ting 5,000 acres in seventy-five days of non-stop harvesting. The fee—sometimes $1.25 per acre—for those performances by "custom threshe.men," independent contractors who owned their own equipment, paid for the machines in a single season!

The prices were extremely expensive for their day, although they reflected both the research and development costs as well as time-payment interest charges included in advance. Holt's engine went for nearly $5,000, his har-

Holt Steamer "Old Betsy"

Holt steam traction engine #1 was built in 1890 and sold for farming. Holt reacquired it circa 1900 and used it around the plant until 1912.

Higgins collection

Compliments of the Photo. Dept.
of THE HOLT MANUFACTURING CO.
Stockton, Calif.

Holt Steamer

Above, this Holt steamer was chained
up to six disk plows near Stockton. In
this configuration, extension rims
were simply another set of rims.
Higgins collection

Holt Steamer and Tricycle Wagons

Right, early Holt steamer stops for a
drink of water on a single track bridge.
Pulling at least three Holt Freight
Company tricycle wagons required a
steady hand and a bit of faith.
Higgins collection

vester for another $2,500. Best's $4,500 engine's comparable price precluded all but the largest farms from adopting steam power. But cost was not the only drawback.

The tractors' outrageous widths made maneuvering them more difficult than managing two or three dozen horses. What's more, horses did not spit glowing embers. Harvesting at night by the light of kerosene lanterns sometimes degenerated into a fireworks show, even with a screen box spark arrestor fitted to the smokestacks. It became a serious enough risk that California's insurers charged a $50 per acre premium during the harvesting of exceptionally dry wheat.

Fire danger was matched by the risk of explosion. Tired engineers, worn out by long days and the relentless heat of the boiler and the sun, sometimes allowed pressure to build too high or water levels to drop too low. Explosions resulted in dozens of deaths and led to California and Oregon legislation regulating boiler construction.

Benjamin and Charles Holt's business grew enough that they purchased a satellite factory in Walla Walla, Washington, in 1902, primarily for the manufacture of the side-hill harvesters. By this time, Benjamin was already concerned about the value of farming the river bottom land in the San Joaquin Valley. He and Charles owned acreage on Roberts Island not far from Stockton. Benjamin knew that his 46ft-wide steamers were too heavy and too inefficient, but that anything narrower or with less support could sink irretrievably into the spongy soil.

He was already aware of tractors on tracks. What's more, with link belts and toothed gears driving his combines and propelling his steamers as well as the belts from his father's lumber mill, Holt was clever enough to imagine broader uses for belts. In 1903, Benjamin and his nephew, Pliny E. Holt, toured Europe and the United States to see what other inventors had created.

The earliest creators of Tracklayers had developed them for reasons similar to those driving Benjamin Holt's curiosity. More than seventy-five years before the Holts' journey, Sir George Cayley received a patent in Great Britain in December 1825, for "an endless chain belt over the two wheels on each side of a wagon." This was meant to support the wagon over soft ground. Seven years later, another Englishman, John Heathcoate, applied Cayley's ideas to a thirty-ton steamer he owned. Heathcoate used belts 7ft-wide on either side and set out to plow a swamp. But the steamer sunk—also sinking his $12,000 experiment. The concept of Tracklayers and flotation still needed work.

Another Englishman, James Boydell, fitted six large, flat, wooden platforms to each of the four wheels of his steamer. These platforms were hinged at the track and came together like a nut cracker. Boydell's innovation in 1846 met with mixed success. It worked, noisily, until the tracks jammed with mud or the pivots froze on icy terrain.

Further development froze as well. Onlookers, skeptical of failures they'd already seen, were reluctant to invest in further experiments by Heathcoate or Boydell. In California twelve years later, that same skepticism limited resources for a further-advanced attempt. In 1858, a year before Daniel Best headed West and seven years before Charles Holt arrived in San Francisco, Warren Miller of Marysville demonstrated his own track-type steam plow at the California State Fair. He won a gold medal and cash, and his machine was patented. However, only one was ever constructed. Miller's machine featured independently driven tracks, which enabled the steamer to be steered easily. Miller's track rollers and tensioners presaged the designs of nearly every crawler to follow. However, the lack of resources limited his future and those who followed him until the turn of the century.

Alvin O. Lombard, a millwright from Waterville, Maine, began building his first "Logging Engine" Tracklayer in 1900. Lombard's design clearly reflected some of Miller's developments, and Lombard's patent application mentioned his Californian predecessor. With a specific need to haul out trees during the winter in mind, he tested it for the rest of the summer, plowing and disking on his 640-acre farm.

For winter use, Lombard fitted sleds to the steering axle. In later years, it dragged out 40,000 board feet of logs

on sleds in one trip—that also brought out huge crowds to see the load. Lombard had received a patent for his machine in 1901 and produced three in the next three years, selling them for $5,000 each. The Eau Claire Mills & Supply Company lumber mill in Eau Claire, Wisconsin, bought the third, then promptly established a subsidiary, Phoenix Manufacturing, and bought the rights to produce Lombard's crawler under license. Phoenix paid the inventor a $1,000 royalty on each one of the sixty-five copies that it produced over the next decade. In 1905, Lombard's own improvements were patented, and by 1915, between the inventor and Phoenix, more than 200 Lombard machines had been sold.

One of the improved models was sold to Western Lumber Company in Lathrop, Montana. It was Lombard's "Improved Log Hauler" that Ben C. Holt, Benjamin's nephew, saw at one of Western's camps. The young engineer from the Spokane branch watched it work, then sent for Uncle

Holt Steamer

A Holt steamer harvesting near

Stockton. This is one of the legendary

46ft rims for flotation in the softest peat.

Higgins collection

George Cabral: Starting a Four-Horse Team

Horses:
Left: Tom, 18.2 hands, 2200lb, 7yr.
Left center: Prince, 17.3 hands, 1900lb, 4yr.
Right center: Don, 173. hands, 1950lb. 5yr.
Right: Jerry, 18.1 hands, 2100lb, 7yr.
All are Black Percherons; Tom and Jerry are the "wheel horses."
The current cost of a good trained Belgian or Percheron is $2,000–$5,000.

1. The night before, check out the equipment that will be used the next day. Be sure that it functions and is greased and that all the equipment is prepared.
2. At sunrise, lead the horses from their mangers, tie them up, and feed them 2lb of grain each, as well as three flakes of oats or hay. Then eat your breakfast.
3. After breakfast, brush the horses down, using a curry brush. Pay particular attention to their shoulders, as this is where the collar rests and is where there will be strain. Check the horses' shoes and feet.
4. After thoroughly brushing them, pad the collars and place them on each horse and attach the harnesses. Brush the horses' shoulders again if necessary to be sure that neither hair nor dirt can accumulate under the collars to hurt the horse.
5. Pair the horses up. Finish the harnessing.
6. When all four—or six, depending on the job—horses are harnessed, remove their halters and fit their bridles. Remove the halters to eliminate the extra weight from the horse's head. Very well-trained horses are accustomed to standing and some do not even need to be tied up at this point.
7. Lead the pairs out and hitch them up for morning. Up to this point, with two men who know what they're doing, this process has taken 30 minutes not including breakfast. It takes another 10 minutes to hitch four horses to the Russell Grader.
8. Work for a couple of hours. Pay attention to the work the horses are doing and to their physical condition. If the work is hard—ripping 20in deep, for example—and they are tired and sweaty, give the horses frequent breaks. A 20in ripper pulls the heck out of six horses or a Fordson 8N in low gear. If the load is not that heavy—light grading with the wheeled Russell Grader, for example—work until noon. Break for lunch.
9. Return to the farm. Unhitch the horses individually and walk them to the mangers. Tie them up, bridles off and halters on. Allow each horse no more than two or three sips of water. Feed them. Then eat lunch. After lunch break, give the horses all the water they want. Remove the halters, replace the bridles, hitch them up, and go back to work.
10. At the end of the day, return with the horses to the yard. Leave the halters on, and take the bridles off. Tie the horses up so that they do not drink yet. Unharness the horses, clean the pads and collars, and put them away. Groom the horses again. If the horses have been working hard, wash their shoulders with salty water to harden their skin. Finish all the tack and equipment cleaning and put it away. After about an hour, release the horses into the corral and turn them lose for they day. At this point, they can drink as much as they wish.

Benjamin to come look at it. A draftsman came along to make drawings and measurements to take back to Stockton.

Benjamin Holt had continued to wonder and worry about his harvesters and tricycle steamers. The heavy machines bogged down in the San Joaquin and Sacramento Rivers' delta. He had heard stories of his tractors—and of Daniel Best's—sinking from sight in the reclaimed marsh lands south of Sacramento.

G. B. Walker, Caterpillar's advertising department manager immediately after the 1925 consolidation, drafted a brief history of the company in 1926. He recreated an enjoyable version of the history of the crawler, while curiously leaving out any reference to other inventors' prior efforts:

"'Do you remember Grandfather's treadmill?' Benjamin Holt asked his nephew and engineer, Pliny E. Holt.

"'Yes,' the younger answered.

"'I believe that treadmills built under the combined harvester wheels would bear it up in the tules just like platforms,' the inventor mused." [Tules, actually varieties of cattails and bulrushes found in marshlands, eventually came to refer to the marshes themselves.]

"'Let's try,' suggested the younger man."

Walker went on to describe the invention:

"Two malleable link belts served as the endless tracks. To these were attached hardwood blocks at regular intervals to serve as treads. The drive wheels were removed from

Circa 1889 Holt Junior Steamer

Left, Holt's first steam wagon used the 40hp junior steam engine. The operator rode ahead of the water tank. It was used primarily for freighting supplies around yard.

Holt Steamer

Far left, freighting to California oil fields from Sacramento Oilwell Supply Company. Holt steamer #118 was the 118th of 133 built. Jervis Eastman photograph

Holt Steamers and Harvesters

Below, seven combined harvesters for seven steamers line up to do battle with the records books at Kern County Land Company's Bakersfield ranch. They cut, threshed, and sacked an acre of standing grain every minute and a half, 32 acres an hour. Higgins collection

Holt Steam tractor No. 77 and the platform wheels were attached over big drive sprockets and idlers. The work was necessarily slow so that the machine was not ready for [field] trial until the early spring of 1905…. Floppety-flop [went] the loose 'platform wheels.' Clickety-click went the long spans of link belting. But it was a principle, not a mechanically perfect machine that Benjamin Holt was proving that day. It worked! It laid its broad tracks right over the soft, bottomless peat lands, bearing up the enormous weight of a big steam engine."

Holt historian Reynold Wik surmised, surely more accurately, that because Holt knew of Lombard and the other tracked efforts, he adapted his own steam engine to tracks. But Walker went on to explain that in the fall of 1904, Benjamin Holt assembled a second rear-tracked machine using his 40hp Junior Road engine. Each "platform

*Holt Junior Steamer
and Lumber Wagons*

*Freighting lumber out of Red River
Lumber, a Holt Junior steamer, #49,
tugs six Holt-built lumber wagons.*

Jervis Eastman photograph

wheel"—or track—was 9ft long and 2ft wide, and consisted of 2x4s attached to one of his link chains so that drive sprockets would engage and move the chains.

"Its performance," Walker wrote, "was tested in comparison with that of a sixty horsepower round wheeler. The bigger engine was loaded to capacity with a fifteen-bottom plow, but the smaller track-type machine pulled a twenty-bottom plow with ease."

It was on Thanksgiving, November 24, 1904, that the steam crawler was first tested—and it is now a well-known story. Holt stood watching it with two friends, a painter, John Shepard, and a photographer, Charles Clements. Holt hired Clements for much of his catalog and documentation work. Clements viewed the scene through his focusing ground glass, seeing the whole thing upside down, the image inverted by the lens. He was briefly hypnotized by the motion of the track undulating between the drive gear and front idler wheel. When he emerged from beneath his black focusing cloth, he observed aloud that Holt's tracks crawled like a caterpillar. Holt took to the name immediately.

Within days, Holt moved the test to Mormon Slough, a boggy area of Stockton just opposite the Houser & Haines subsidiary. In the mud and grass, the new "caterpillar" performed with no recorded problems. From there, it was hauled quickly to Roberts Island, where Benjamin and Charles' land would become tillable for the first time thanks to the success of their crawler. The second test prototype, assembled on the chassis of no. 77 with a Holt 40hp Junior Road engine, led to more tests. In all, six prototypes were assembled and put through a variety of field work in 1905 and 1906. At the end of 1906, the seventh Holt Brothers Paddle Wheel Improved Traction Engine, no. 111,—Holt's first production model—was shipped to J. M. Jefferey's Golden Meadow Development Company. This was a satisfied customer's repeat business. Golden Meadow already owned one of Holt's large round wheel steamers, and was reclaiming and clearing land in Lockport, Louisiana, LaFourche Parish (roughly forty-five miles southwest of New Orleans), in a boggy area destined for sugar cane.

Holt Junior Steamer

Holt Junior steamer #53 with Holt harvester worked in the rice north of Sacramento. Higgins collection

Chapter 3

Slow Progress

*The Search for New Fuels ✦ Best Manufacturing Company
Incorporated in 1893 ✦ Early Best Gas Engines ✦ Holts Found Aurora Engine
Company in 1906 ✦ Best Sells Out to Holt ✦ The Holt Caterpillar Company
Founded in 1908 ✦ Northern Holt Company Founded in 1909*

Best 60 in the Hollywoodland Hills

1909 Holt Model 45B

"Northern Holt"

Opposite page, the Northern Holt

Company licensed Minneapolis'

Diamond Iron Works to produce

redesigned Holt crawlers for Midwest

farmers. Only two were completed.

This one—#102—was sold for

$3,000 to a Mexican plantation.

Engineers and tractor makers in America and Europe knew that steam power was inefficient. Its shortcomings and dangers were well known. But it wasn't until oil was discovered and its vapor utilized first as lamp fuel and then as an engine fuel that serious and practical alternatives to steam were realistic goals. Engineers began experiments in France and Germany in the early 1860s. By 1890, the courts in Europe ordered the patented four-cycle gasoline-burning engines of Nikolaus Otto into the public domain. It was too valuable an improvement, the courts decided, to keep restricted any longer. From that point, its development spread like the very vapors it consumed and exhausted.

The *Pacific Rural Press* in September 1891 announced that Best's "electric crude oil vapor engine" was awarded first premium at the State Fair. "This engine," it reported, "can be operated on either crude oil, distillate, gasoline, or kerosene. It is the cheapest power on earth."

Terry Galloway quoted Daniel Best's observations: "A test with one of our five horsepower crude oil engines, running ten hours on different gas oils showed California crude oil to be the most economical; it took seven-and-one-half gallons of forty gravity oil at five cents per gallon."

Best's gas engines worked first for electric power generation at his own plant and at a competitor's, H. G. Shaw Plow Works. Shaw produced straw-burner portable steam power units. By 1892, Best had produced two-cylinder, 16hp units for street cars in San Jose. But these were big units. A sales brochure detailed the vital statistics: The "duplex" street car unit weighed 2850lb and occupied 19x60in of floor space. Each cylinder measured 8x10in bore and stroke to produce 16hp at 230rpm. It required a 60gal water tank on each car for engine cooling. And it sold for $1,200, including delivery and set up.

On January 23, 1893, Best incorporated the Best Manufacturing Company, reflecting, as Benjamin Holt had done, the changes in technology and the broadening scope of his operations. Street cars did not fit agricultural works.

Best continued development work on gas engines and by late June, he was ready to show off his "oil vapor traction engine," a gasoline tractor. He chained one of his steamers to his new gas tractor for a tug-of-war. Even with a full head of steam, the 50hp steamer—which actually produced 110hp—was pulled backwards around the block, towed easily by the new machine. Best applied for a patent for his gas tractor three months later.

According to Galloway, Best's first gasoline tractor bore a strong visual resemblance to his big steamers. However, they also featured some interesting innovations: "The electric oil vapor engine consists of two two-cylinder engines coupled together. Two of the pistons may be disconnected by a simple coupling from the crank for light loads, or they can be operated in unison for heavy loads. Above the motor is shown the large vertical assembly which consists of a carburetor that generates the combustible hydrocarbon vapor. The vapor is heated by a head exchanging with the hot exhaust gases for greater efficiency of operation. The drivetrain has a differential, a clutch, and a reversing gear. Its wheels are all spring-mounted to absorb the shocks of rough ground."

Best also became interested in the automobile, producing two models. The most well known was an open carriage with seating for eight, powered by a smaller, lighter version of his 7hp opposed two-cylinder. This pushed the 2570lb machine to 18mph fully loaded, or stretched out about 150 miles of travel at more reasonable speeds. Galloway quoted Best's recollections:

"Well, I was smitten with the automobile fever, and accordingly set about to construct one. I tell you, that automobile was a work of art—in my own opinion—with all the grace of a mud scow," Best explained. Built in nine days, he used it for eleven years. "I constructed a second machine, a two-passenger, and later gave it to my son. He in turn traded it for a piano. I think the piano man was cheated.

"I have often thought that if I had stayed with automobile manufacturing, I could have out-Forded Ford. Perhaps."

**Starting the Holt 25hp Model 40,
Serial Number #1004, with Aurora
Gasoline Engine**

1. Fill the fuel tank with gasoline or distillate.
2. Check the oil level in the mechanical oiler mounted at the head of the engine.
3. Fill oil boxes on each rear deck that lubricate the chains that drive sprockets.
4. Set the throttle lever to about one-third open.
5. Set the magneto timing slightly advanced.
6. Open the compression release valves.
7. Open the priming cups.
8. Set the magneto impulse lever.
9. Prime each cylinder profusely.
10. Close all priming cups.
11. Stand over the driveshaft facing the flywheel, with the driveshaft guard in place.
12. Grasp the flywheel with your hands. Turn until you have reached the top dead center of the compression stroke.
13. Crank vigorously.
14. If the engine fails to start, repeat this procedure from steps 7 to 13 as many times as necessary. When the engine starts, close the compression release valves.
15. Adjust the throttle to idle.
16. Adjust the magneto timing.
17. Check the oiler dripping sequence to be certain that enough oil is passing to the bearings.
18. Check water flow through the sight glass above the radiator.
19. Check the gasoline fuel pump packing gland to prevent air leaks.
20. As the engine warms up to operating temperature, screw down grease cup caps to grease track rollers and transmission gears.
21. Once the engine has reached operating temperature, disengage the clutch, and select first gear. Smoothly release the clutch and go.

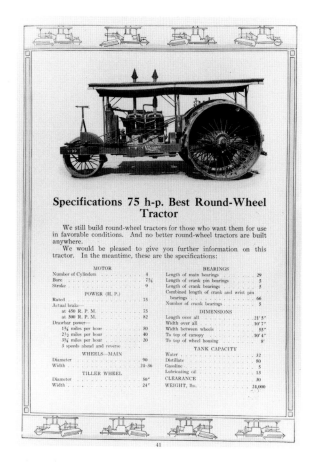

the first decade of the Twentieth Century. Best had already been awarded thirty patents and another half dozen were still to come. Revenue for 1905 was reported at $300,000 and sales of harvesters and steamers to Australia accounted for some of that success. But gasoline engines still amounted to experiments.

A year later, in early October 1906, Benjamin and Pliny Holt organized the Aurora Engine Company in Stockton. Many of Holt's stockholders remained resolutely unconvinced of the value of unproven gas engines and they were wary of their development costs. But both Benjamin and Pliny were certain that the future led away from steam; the Aurora Engine Company gave the men the chance to develop the engines away from the scrutiny and dividend-consciousness of their investors.

The technology, of course, was well established. Reynold Wik characterized it in his book, *Benjamin Holt & Caterpillar*: "When the decision was made to turn to gasoline engines, all that was required were changes in blueprints and the building and mounting of gasoline motors on existing chassis which had previously carried the boilers of steam traction engines. As a result, the conversion in farm machinery from steam to gasoline power occurred quickly, and the new industry was launched almost full grown."

The Holts had their first gas-engined Caterpillar in field tests as early as December 1906. Within two years, regular production began and in 1908, four were produced and sold. One went to Charles Lamb, a farmer in nearby Galt, thirty miles north. This was the first agricultural application for a gasoline crawler tractor.

The first three went to supplement the Holt steam tractors already in use on the Los Angeles Aqueduct project. In 1908, Los Angeles voters funded a $23 million bond issue to bring water 225 miles from central California's Owens River south to Los Angeles. A concrete aqueduct was to be

His son, the pianist, was twenty-year-old C. L., who had been named superintendent of the plant only four months earlier.

Sales of steam traction engines and combined harvesters and of Best's own side-hill harvesters continued into

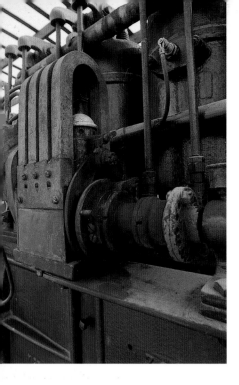

1908 Holt 25hp Model 40

Above, using an American Bosch magneto, the Holt 6.00x7.00in bore-and-stroke four-cylinder engine ran at 650rpm. A Schebler 1.5in single-barrel carburetor fed the gas engine.

Best 75hp Tracklayer

Far right, Combination phantom drawing and cutaway of the Best 75hp Tracklayer. Higgins collection

1908 Holt 25hp Model 40

Right, Ben Holt's belief in link-belts extended to the use of chain to direct the front steering tiller wheel. However, a worm-and-sector gearbox translated the steering wheel's directions to the chain. The front wheel is 3ft tall, 1ft wide.

constructed over several mountain ranges and through the Mojave Desert. City Engineer William Mulholland heard about Holt's steam engines on tracks and ordered one. Holt's 100hp steamer easily proved up to the task of hauling as much as thirty-one tons up a steady 14 percent grade. Initial enthusiasm prompted orders for a total of twenty-eight tractors over six months. Holt's factory went into second shifts to produce the machines.

But the desert and the mountains offered different challenges from the San Joaquin River delta's soft soil. Even though the steamers were fired by crude oil carried in on-board tanks, water for the boilers had to be transported a long way. Dust and heat took their toll. Repairs to the steamers were so frequent and so expensive—in time out of service and in material costs—that on some stretches of the project, Mulholland reverted to using mules—until the arrival of Holt's gasoline-engined machines.

Holt himself viewed the entire project as a thorough experiment and development exercise. Cast-iron gears wore out from abrasion by the sand, and Holt replaced them with steel castings. The brutal terrain broke suspension springs and burned up the two-speed transmissions whose low gear simply was not low enough for some of the climbs. Modifications were done at the factory and in the desert to remedy each newly discovered problem. But in an era seventy years before computer-aided design and manufacture and before overnight air delivery, parts replacement became another source of friction between the customer and manufacturer. Benjamin and Pliny Holt visited the desert and with Russell Springer, Holt's factory shop manager, set up repair facilities in the work camps. They offered even exchange for tractors needing overhaul and furnished more spare parts and more mechanics to the sites.

Mulholland was a strong believer in machinery and in the end, the gas tractors mostly fulfilled his expectations. While his final report after the 1913 completion of the aqueduct labeled the Holt tractors as the only unsatisfactory purchase for the project, he actually found ways to recycle the machines: "The gas engines [were] taken from there for uses in places where gasoline power was desirable. The frame work of some of these engines was used for steel forms for concrete work, and some 'Caterpillars' were sold to private parties for farming purposes."

The keen competition between Benjamin Holt and Daniel Best led first to a lawsuit filed in 1905 by Best against Holt, charging infringement on Best's patents. Best had developed the first power take-off by running live steam from the engine on his traction engine through flexible tubing to a second engine bolted onto his harvester.

Holt's defense was that he had placed an auxiliary engine on the rear of his steam tractor. Witnesses testified that Holt's system broke whenever the tractor negotiated tight turns or moved over uneven terrain, and so this system was upgraded in 1904. Holt's "upgrade" placed the auxiliary engine on the harvester, where Best's was located.

1908 Holt 25hp Model 40

Above, this unusual engine block configuration featured box-like oil reservoirs beneath each cylinder. The four cylinders were cast en-bloc with the heads welded onto the cylinders.

Best 70hp Round-Wheel Tractor

Left, later production 70hp round-wheel tractors utilized increased frame support. The worm-roller-and-chain steering absorbed shock but was imprecise. Higgins collection

Right, Pliny Holt's "Northern Holt" 45 contrasts dramatically with the Stockton Model 45s. It included a belt pulley wheel, in the shadow of the canopy and awning. Measuring 8ft wide without awnings, it is 9ft-8in tall. This unique example belongs to Fred Heidrick, Sr.

Holt lost, but on appeal he pointed out that each significant feature of Best's harvester had first appeared on George Berry's combine. The first case went to trial in November 1907 and was settled a month later. The appeal was filed in May 1908, and in August a circuit court judge overturned the ruling, sending it to lower court for retrial.

But it never got there. Outside of the courtroom, the two sides had begun talking peace. Or, more accurately, acquisition.

Daniel Best was now seventy years old. On October 8, 1908, he sold his business to Benjamin and Charles Holt for $750,000. Both sides had already experimented with gasoline-burning engines and they saw that the end of steam power was looming. Each side had also supported lawyers for several years. They agreed to settle, to combine their assets and liabilities, their dealers and technologies, and to operate together under the name of The Holt Manufacturing Company.

Best's attorney, Henry C. "Monty" Montgomery, explained the behind-the-scenes dealings years later. He participated in the negotiations leading to the settlement: "I came in on the tail end of that suit as junior partner for the law firm handling Best's case. Holt took an appeal but [his] lawyers worked up a settlement to give Best $35,000 and started negotiations to purchase Best for Holt.

"The deal went through, and Old Man Best gave C. L. one-third interest in stock [in Best Manufacturing], with

1908 Holt 25hp Model 40

Left, five truck rollers supported the Holt crawler. Tracks were 15.5x10in steel.

C. L. Best 40hp Round-Wheel Tractor

Below, an early round-wheel tractor featured an interesting rear wheel brake—that slim band around the drive wheel. Higgins collection

Daniel Best Street Car Motor

Upper right, Daniel Best's opposed two-cylinder 16hp street car engine used a 3ft-diameter flywheel. Higgins collection

1909 Holt Model 45B
"Northern Holt"

Right, Pliny Holt replaced the front tiller wheel with a pair of narrow steel wheels, meant to make the Caterpillar appear more normal to Midwestern farmers.

Holt Prototype

Below, this Holt Mystery Machine was photographed in back of Fred Grimsley's shops. Grimsley was Holt's Los Angeles branch agent. This was likely Grimsley's rotary plow. Higgins collection

two-thirds going to Holt…. C. L. went in as president of the revamped corporation, but Holt had control."

Holt's desire to get on with business and to expand its markets was evident by its attempts in Seattle and Minneapolis. Early in 1908 a branch sales office was established in Seattle to augment harvester sales generated directly from the Walla Walla factory. During the Los Angeles aqueduct project in 1909, Pliny Holt opened The Northern Holt Company office to produce tractors in Minneapolis, where he had studied engineering at the University of Minnesota. Pieces for the assembly of ten of the company's 25hp Model 45 B gasoline-powered crawler tractors were shipped to Minneapolis for assembly at the Diamond Iron Works under license from Holt. Two of these were completed. Pliny had "redesigned" these tractors for Midwestern farmers. He had specified two front steering wheels connected by a fixed shaft through the usual rotating drum that had housed one wider wheel in the Western versions. In addition, he added a side-mounted drive pulley for belt work. But crawler tractors offered less of an advantage over wheel-type tractors in Midwestern soils, and these Holts were priced nearly $1,000 more than their competitors. In the end, only one of the two assembled tractors sold, and Pliny was forced to take it back because the farmer was dissatisfied.

While in Minneapolis, however, Pliny Holt met Murray Baker, an implement dealer for the Buffalo Pitts Company, from Peoria, Illinois. Baker, as much a salesman as an independent entrepreneur, knew of a large plant in Illinois whose owner, William Colean, a thresher and steamer

manufacturer, had bankrupted recently. For six months, Baker served as intermediary in the negotiations between Pliny Holt and the bankruptcy court and its bank receiver. There were numerous frustrating and nervous moments, but in the end, on October 25, 1909, Holt had acquired a new home in Peoria. And when the company incorporated in Illinois the following January, it bore a new name, The Holt Caterpillar Company.

1910 Best 75hp Round-Wheel Tractor

In 1909, Theodore Shank bought a gasoline tractor after giving up on steam. This Best round-wheel was sold with a 60hp six-cylinder Buffalo engine.

1910 Best 75hp Round-Wheel Tractor

Right, "The (60hp) motor wasn't strong enough," Shank explained in the late 1960s. "We put a Best (75hp) engine into this tractor. We cut the frame off and spliced in about seven inches so this new engine would fit." The plow-shaped deflector was factory original. It kept the fan or the radiator's air from affecting the number-one cylinder's performance. Bottom right, Shank used his 75hp round-wheel until he died in 1971, farming as many as 1,400 acres in desert heat as high as 127 degrees Fahrenheit. Best's own four-cylinder engine, introduced in 1911, measured 7.75x9.00in bore and stroke and was rated at 82hp at 500rpm.

Holt Prototype

Opposite page, this Holt Mystery Machine may be the first Holt gasoline engine tractor, from 1905. These also may be a custom Holt gas engine built on order for a vineyard owner, Mr. Wheeler, north of Sacramento. While its purpose is unknown, it used many pieces from Holt's steamer plus the engine from the Samson Sieve Grip tractor.

Higgins collection

1910 Best 75hp Round-Wheel Tractor

Previous page, this round-wheel was the 51st produced. Overall it stands 21ft-5in long, 10ft-7in wide, and 10ft-4in tall. Its lineage from Dan Best's steamers is easy to see. Shank's son David, of Scottsdale, Arizona, owns this tractor, believed to be the only 75hp round-wheel in existence.

1921 Russell Grader

Right, up until the early 1920s, earth moving was a slow, back-breaking task even with the improvements of horsepower and wheeled road graders. At about 1mph, George Cabral and Paul Reno improve the road alongside the fields.

Russell Motor Patrol and Holt 2-Ton

Right, a future motor grader operator watches from the side of the road. The Russell Motor Patrol blade and front end were mounted on a Holt 2-Ton crawler. Higgins collection

1921 Russell Grader

Left, George Cabral drives his four-horsepower Russell road grader along the orchard road near home in Ceres, California. His Black Percherons—from left, Jerry, Don, Prince, and Tom—barely break a sweat crowning an aggregate and dirt path.

1921 Russell Grader

Below, Paul Reno adjusts the grader blade as George Cabral calls the horses to work. The working horses steam in the cold air. Cabral's draft horses, each weighing nearly 2,000lb, primarily demonstrate older farming techniques rather than still performing them.

Chapter 4

War I: In Court

C. L. Best Breaks Away ✦ *C. L. Best Gas Traction Company Created in 1910* ✦
"Best in the Business" ✦ *Holt Registers "Caterpillar" Trademark in 1910* ✦
Patent Battles ✦ *The Black Book Findings*

1922 Best 60 Tracklayer

Above, fill 'er up. This Best 60
Tracklayer was fitted with auxiliary
track pads but it was still hard on
paved streets. Higgins collection

1917 Best 75hp Tracklayer

Laurence Darrach's Best 75hp
Tracklayer has been in his family since
1917. The 28,000lb, 23ft-9in-long
machine was in regular use until the
mid-1960s. At present, only a handful
are known to exist.

C. L. Best stayed with the Holt operations in his father's old shops in San Leandro until early 1910. C. L. was a competent businessman in his own right and a clever enough marketer, but most of all he was an innovative engineer. While he was the president of the San Leandro subsidiary on paper, however, the rivalry between the Holts and Bests had continued, and many of C. L.'s ideas were thwarted by Holt family members, who were in subordinate roles at San Leandro but held seats on Holt's Board of Directors. In addition, Holt had given signature rights to Best's treasurer that made him equal to Best.

Although the terms of his father's 1908 sale prohibited C. L. from returning to the tractor business for ten years, he resettled in Elmhurst, near San Leandro, and began to produce wheeled and crawler tractors. C. L.'s new company was called the C. L. Best Gas Traction Company. It came as a surprise to no one.

"C. L. didn't get along," Henry Montgomery explained. "He came to me in about 1910 and wanted out of the deal. He had to lose what cash he had in the old firm, but Daniel Best financed C. L., and he started up at Elmhurst."

The C. L. Best Gas Traction Company was founded on about $80,000 from Daniel Best, with about $25,000 from C. L.'s brother-in-law, Charles Q. Nelson, a farmer in Woodland, and another $75,000 from other farmers and friends.

"Best began advertising he was the only 'Best in Business,'" Montgomery recalled. "C. L. took most of the key men in the move from San Leandro to Elmhurst to start his new company. Holt soon sued C. L. for infringement on the name. I defended C. L. There was naturally a lot of confusion of mail, telephone and wire orders, callers, etc. [between C. L. Best Gas Traction Company formerly of San Leandro and Holt Manufacturing Company still in San Leandro but operating out of Daniel Best's old shops].

"Holt hired Townsend, one of San Francisco's big names in patent law. He had 400 pages of affidavits. I de-

fended C. L. on the grounds [that] he had something entirely new, as his firm name indicated—gas.

"Holt," Montgomery continued, "still had a big steam outfit; Best, a small gasoline rig. We licked 'em. It cost Holt a lot.

"C. L. was cocky now. He started building the track-type [tractors]. The demand for crawler tractors was coming up strong. At the 1915 California State Fair, C. L. demonstrated his crawler. It made Holt mad. He sued."

Holt had a lot on his mind, a lot to be angry about. Communication with his nephew's new factory 2,000 miles away in Peoria was slow by mail and expensive by telephone. The financially costly breakdowns on the Los Angeles aqueduct project in the Mojave Desert 200 miles away were damaging his reputation as well. And now he found himself once again in fierce competition with a Best. This Best was barely ten miles away, the son of a former competitor, and former president of his own subsidiary company.

Daniel Best had been producing 50 and 110hp steam traction engines at the turn of the century. A decade later, C. L. was manufacturing 60hp gas tractors. In another year, the 60hp was replaced by an 80hp. And C. L.'s first crawler, the 75hp, was introduced a year after that, in 1912.

Best's tractors appeared in black paint with gold lettering. There was not much visual contrast to Benjamin Holt's brown tractors with yellow trim, especially when seen from the far side of a field. Best called his crawlers "Tracklayers." Holt had registered Clements' term, "Caterpillar," as a trademark in 1910.

The rivalry continued.

Best's Tracklayers bore remarkable similarity to Holt's Caterpillars. Cautious after the first suit against Best, Holt tried to control the crawler patents. He had his lawyers trace the history and legitimacy of every prior patent, those of George Berry and Alvin O. Lombard in particular. Holt's lawyers advised that there was little value to be gained in buying the Lombard patents outright, and point-

1914 Holt Model 30

Known as the Baby Holt, this Model 30 was introduced in 1914 and within a year was available without its front tiller wheel. As was the practice with many tractor makers, an arrow mounted above the front wheel indicated its direction to an operator.

Starting the Best 75hp Tracklayer

1. Prime the cylinders through the top priming cups, giving each cylinder about two squirts with a gasoline can. Do not overprime.
2. Open the compression relief valves for all cylinders.
3. Open the gas tank safety valve.
4. Trip the impulse starter and advance the spark level to "full."
5. Advance the throttle lever about half way.
6. Start the engine by placing the cranking bar in holds in the flywheel.
7. When the resistance or compression is felt, give the bar a quick pull to bring the crank over dead center quickly.
Note: Do not stand over the bar and do not allow anyone to stand directly opposite the flywheel and bar when cranking. An engine backfire may throw the bar a great distance.
8. As soon as the engine starts, close the compression relief cocks.
9. The engine will start better in cold weather if the gas valve on the carburetor is open one turn and the air valve is entirely closed. The air valve should remain closed at least 30 minutes until the engine heats up. If flames shoot from the exhaust pipes, your mixture is too rich. Proper carburetor adjustment will eliminate this.

ed out that none of Holt's own patents were entirely unique or original. Holt's hope of controlling a monopoly faded but so did his worry of infringement suits.

Or so he thought.

C. L. Best had done his homework as well. Best's attorney, Henry Montgomery, had reached the same conclusions as Holt's lawyers. But Montgomery's advice differed: Purchase any Lombard patents that predated Holt's. Any question of whose work came first would be solved by ownership of the earliest patents.

"That Holt patent no. 874,008, granted in 1907, was the basis of his suit," Montgomery said. "Holt had a hat full of patents and Best [had] none. My search soon convinced me that Alvin O. Lombard of Waterville, Maine, was the key that could whip Holt and turn the tables if we could get it. I got Lombard's address and wrote. He never answered."

Holt's 1907 patent protected him. It described a "Traction Engine—introduction of normal flexibility and resilience of the girdle frame by location of driving and idler sprocket wheels on main frame out of contact with ground; introduction of pair of elevated two-rail tracks with laterally extended tread members for traction and protection; flanged weight-supporting track rollers adapted to travel on the ground reaches of the elevated pair of double tracks of the belt; and substituting gas engine for steam."

"We were right in the middle," Montgomery went on, "with Holt hiring eleven of the top patent lawyers of the

1914 Holt Model 30

Right, the 16in steering wheel required twenty-nine full revolutions to spin the front tiller wheel from stop to stop. But steering clutches and track brakes aided maneuverability. The Baby was 19ft-4in long and 7ft-6in to the top of the tiller wheel arrow.

1914 Holt Model 30

Below, Holt's four-cylinder engine used an American Bosch MJB4-128 magneto for ignition and a Schleber carburetor for fuel mix. The flywheel—its starting rod in it—measured 29in across. Flywheel horsepower was 30 at 650rpm, drawbar rating 20hp.

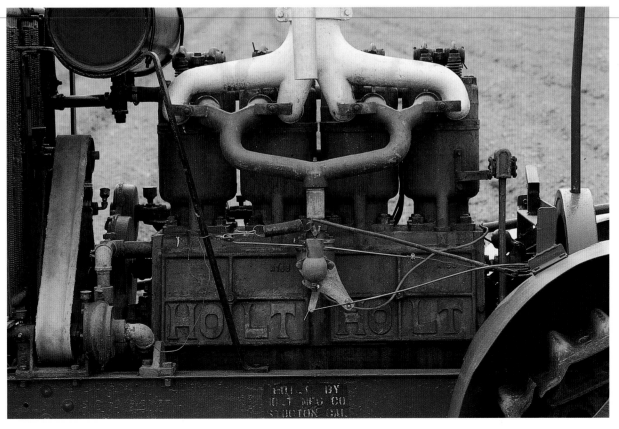

1914 Holt Model 30

Right, Holt's 13x12in steel tracks reportedly generated barely 7psi of ground force. Improvements in design fitted three truck rollers over the track length and two track carrier rollers on top to support the tracks.

1917 Holt Model 75 and Holt Land Leveller Scraper

Bottom left, the Holt Model 75 1400ci four-cylinder engine used a K-W high-tension magneto on the 7.50x8.00in cylinders. Holt rated the engine at 75hp at 550rpm. The engine could idle slowly enough that a listener can count the individual revolutions.

C. L. Best 75hp Tracklayer

Far right, this was not a demonstration stunt: the 75hp Tracklayers were so heavy that they regularly broke wooden bridges. Dave Smith collection

United States: Fish of Boston, Rector of Toledo Scale, Church of Washington, DC, and International Harvester's best man.

"I was with Old Man Scribner, nearly eighty, so the burden was on me. I said to Best, 'Lombard's patent is your best defense!'"

Montgomery took the next train across country to Maine to see Lombard. He had been manufacturing crawlers for fifteen years. Lombards were all over the woods from Maine to Montana and up into Canada.

"By God, young man, I'm glad to meet you," Montgomery reported that Lombard said to him. "If God

almighty would charter me to kill a man, I'd get on a train, go out to California, and kill old Benjamin Holt!"

Montgomery learned that in late 1910, just after Best separated from Holt, Lombard had gone out to California and called on both manufacturers to discuss their crawlers and his patents. Best was out of the city, and for some reason, Lombard couldn't or didn't wait. He got a tour of the Holt plant and a promise from the older Holt to send Pliny back with a payment and a licensing agreement. But for some reason, Pliny was called back to Stockton. Lombard considered this a brush off.

Montgomery concluded that Lombard was a brilliant

engineer but, "being too stingy to hire a lawyer, he had been boiling all these years since Holt started building crawlers."

Montgomery trailed an early Lombard steam crawler out to Montana, to Western Logging Company's manager Charles Richardson, who remembered the Holts' visit to examine his Lombard Log Hauler.

"So I began talking to Lombard about coming out to testify," Montgomery went on. "We finally convinced the old man and his daughter, Mrs. Vose, to come out for the San Francisco World's Fair; we'd pay their expenses and he'd testify, too."

In the US District Court for Northern California, Best

1917 Holt Model 75 and Holt Land Leveller Scraper

Even with Holt's patented track clutches and brakes, cutting a tight turn on a tiller-wheel Caterpillar takes quick reactions and elbow grease, as Bill Cox demonstrates. Operating Don Hunter's Model 75 looks easier than it is.

1917 Holt Model 75 and

Holt Land Leveller Scraper

"Do Not Overload," Holt's owners manual warned. "Be guided by the equivalent number of horses required to pull the equipment that is place behind the 'Caterpillar' Tractor." It's difficult to imagine what it would take to overload the 75hp "Caterpillar."

and Montgomery accused Holt of infringement of Lombard's patents. Holt's lawyers cross-examined Lombard, who, in concluding his testimony, threatened to sue Holt himself. After that day's session, Montgomery approached Lombard. The older inventor then sold his two primary patents to C. L. Best for $20,000. And then Best counter-sued Holt.

"Best was a small corporation, with just about $70,000 paid in and it was well extended," Montgomery explained. "Old Man Best had to bail the little company out now and then. I told C. L., 'I've got 'em buffaloed now. I can get you some dough. Get licenses and we can make some real dough!'

"'Get me $50,000, and a license to use all the patents, and I'll be satisfied,' said C. L.

"I went up to Stockton and stayed for four days. I came out with $200,000 in cash and a license. It put Best on his feet for the first time."

Montgomery suddenly found himself with the reputation as the patent authority on crawler tractors. The junior partner, freshly graduated from the University of Michigan Law School, had used his thoroughness and resourcefulness and had toppled the established names in his field. Holt retained him immediately after losing the lawsuit to Best. "We transferred the Lombard patents to Holt. Then Holt hired me to go out over the United States and license all other track builders: Monarch, Bates, Cletrac. I had the job for three years. It was license or sue, until they were all paying Holt royalties of $25 to $100 per tractor for building crawlers."

Despite all of the challenges to Benjamin Holt—the aqueduct and his expensive battles in the courtrooms—Holt's company emerged as one of the fortunate few in 1914 and 1915. The high repair costs that Holt had to absorb in the Mojave Desert were offset by more than

$140,000 in revenues from the project. And the tractors, forced to improve by the uncharitable conditions there, shed weak, brittle cast iron for steel components throughout. Holt adopted better suspensions, stronger clutches, and three-speed transmissions, and the tractors became much more durable. Hundreds of other tractor makers in the Midwest and East went out of business at this time; factory-paid repairs to primitive machines—and the bad reputations that accompanied them—bankrupted the others. Holt endured, and became stronger than ever.

Oscar Starr, who eventually became director of engineering at Caterpillar Tractor Company, worked for both Holt and Best in the earliest days. He joined Holt's Aurora Engine Company in April 1912.

Hal Higgins, Caterpillar's communications director, spent more than thirty years starting in the late 1920s interviewing dozens of Best, Holt, and Caterpillar employees during and after their careers. It was Higgins' intention,

even after his retirement in 1952, to gather together as much of the company's history as possible from those who had made it.

"At the Aurora works," Starr explained to Higgins, "I found a few good tools and they were fooling around…with no one knowing how to operate what they had. The problem was production. They wanted to build two engines a day. I soon got production up to three engines a day.

"Early in 1913, the Aurora gas engine was good enough that they decided to take it into the Holt Company. When Benjamin Holt came home from his world tour [demonstrating and selling tractors in Russia and central Europe], I had about 300 Aurora engines stacked up outside the plant at Stockton. I had asked how many they wanted before he left and had been given a go-ahead for all I could produce. So there were engines running out their ears when they returned," Starr said.

1917 Holt Model 75 and

Holt Land Leveller Scraper

Holt's open-front land levellers resembled scrapers made by T. G. Schmeiser. Holt's version rose and fell only from the center. A large drum provided friction against the broad belt that elevated the scraper blade.

1917 Holt Model 75 and

Holt Land Leveller Scraper

Above and upper right, with its Holt Land Leveller in tow, Don Hunter's 1917 Holt Model 75 is about to begin flattening berms in a 20-acre meadow before plowing and planting. The large wheel controls the height of the scraper bucket through friction on the belts.

1917 Holt 75hp Tracklayer

Right, a fold-out page from Holt's 1917 sales brochure. Higgins collection

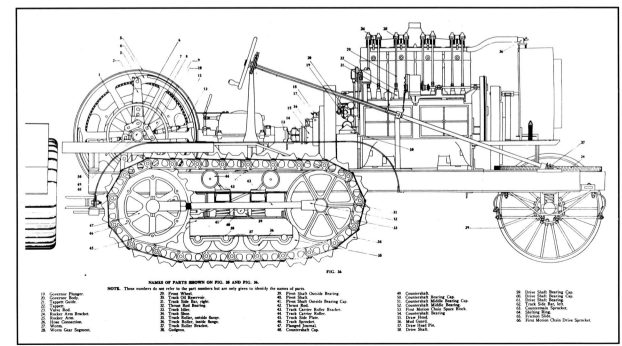

FIG. 36.

NAMES OF PARTS SHOWN ON FIG. 35 AND FIG. 36.

NOTE. These numbers do not refer to the part numbers but are only given to identify the names of parts.

19.	Governor Plunger.	29.	Front Wheel.	39.	Pivot Shaft Outside Bearing.	49. Countershaft.	59. Drive Shaft Bearing Cap.
20.	Governor Body.	30.	Track Oil Reservoir.	40.	Pivot Shaft.	50. Countershaft Bearing Cap.	60. Drive Shaft Bearing Cap.
21.	Tappett Guide.	31.	Track Side Bar, right.	41.	Pivot Shaft Outside Bearing Cap.	51. Countershaft Middle Bearing Cap.	61. Drive Shaft Bearing.
22.	Tappett.	32.	Thrust Rod Bearing.	42.	Thrust Rod.	52. Countershaft Middle Bearing.	62. Track Side Bar, left.
23.	Valve Rod.	33.	Track Idler.	43.	Track Carrier Roller Bracket.	53. First Motion Chain Space Block.	63. Countermain Sprocket.
24.	Rocker Arm Bracket.	34.	Track Shoe.	44.	Track Carrier Roller.	54. Countershaft Bearing.	64. Countermain Sprocket.
25.	Rocker Arm.	35.	Truck Roller, outside flange.	45.	Truck Side Plate.	55. Draw Head.	65. Shifting Ring.
26.	Hose Connection.	36.	Truck Roller, inside flange.	46.	Track Sprocket.	56. Mud Guard.	66. Friction Slide.
27.	Worm.	37.	Truck Roller Bracket.	47.	Flanged Journal.	57. Draw Head Pin.	67. First Motion Chain Drive Sprocket.
28.	Worm Gear Segment.	38.	Gudgeon.	48.	Countershaft Cap.	58. Drive Shaft.	

1913 Best Model 30 "Humpback"
Above, Best kept tractor height low and operator visibility clear even with a tiller steering wheel 15ft away. A complex gear linkage accomplished the task.

1913 Best Model 30 "Humpback"
Left, this configuration was adopted for orchards and groves where overall height was all-important. The "humpback" configuration reappeared when the High Drive models came along in the late 1970s.

"'Jesus Christ, what will we do with all these engines?' Benjamin exclaimed when he saw the pile that accumulated while he was gone.

"We got $400 to $500 each for them in those days. They were in three sizes: seven by eight, six by seven, and a small one. The big one went into the Holt Caterpillars, and the next size went into a smaller 'Cat,' I believe."

Holt's problems with having each of his eight factories independent was becoming apparent.

"I was at Aurora Works about a year," Starr went on. "I didn't like it and came to work for C. L. Best in late 1913. I had never met C. L. until then. I headed Production there. One or two of his Best Tracklayers were in production at the time. Best had so many financial problems at this stage that he wasn't paying much attention to building them. I started with one [tractor produced] a month, soon stepped up to one a week, then two or three a week.

"I guess there were about 100 men in the Best plant at the time. We were paid once a month when Best had the money. Getting the payroll together was a problem that called for selling a tractor or borrowing money."

Philip Rose was an independent tractor engineer, who had taught steam engineering at North Dakota Agricultural College and had edited *American Thresherman* magazine. He was retained by General Motors in 1914 and 1915 to survey all the companies producing tractors in the United States during this time. As GM sought to tap into the market that had been controlled so effectively by Henry Ford, the Detroit conglomerate knew it needed an educated judgment of its potential competition and an assessment of possible acquisition targets.

Rose summarized months of travel and investigation in his *Black Book*. Rose briefly addressed the patent question: "The tracklaying or caterpillar idea is very old and un-

patentable, but several methods of reducing it to practice have been patented by manufacturers, notably Best and Holt. The Patent Office records are valuable in tracing this history."

His assessments of the mechanical differences between the two makers were more decisive: "The Best has developed many refinements which have been thoroughly proved out, while the Holt sticks to the old, conservative design, always trying to improve their materials and methods, but not changing or adding to the mechanism."

Best was reported to be producing one tractor every third day. "The entire West," Rose wrote, "looks on a Best tractor as the automobile public looks at a Packard automobile."

Holt, which operated two factories at the time, portrayed two different markets and gave Rose two distinct impressions. The Peoria operation was managed by a mechanical engineer, E. F. Norelius, about whom Rose could learn little and from whom he learned little more. Norelius did say that "'In 1912, Holt couldn't build tractors big enough; in 1915, they could not build them small enough.'" In mid-1913, Holt began experimenting with two-tread machines to be introduced in 1916. Rose left with an unfavorable opinion of Holt at Peoria and of Norelius. Ironically, Norelius himself left Holt just about a decade later to join Allis-Chalmers, where, among other successes, he designed the Model L crawler, the machine that challenged Best's—and then Caterpillar's Sixty—so effectively that Caterpillar hurried to introduce its Model 70.

In Stockton, Rose had much more access. There he learned that at all three plants—Stockton, Peoria, and in Washington state—Holt employed a total of 800 personnel, producing three tractors a day. "These people are one of the few American firms who have a sympathetic understanding of the export business and its requirements. They believe that the surest way to increase business is by ample financing. This means that the customer frequently earns with his engine the wherewithal to pay for it."

Rose went on to describe the contrasts between Best's drive system using a differential and Holt's, which "drives each side separately and eliminates the differential." Best, he commented, had "a huge differential, which enables them to pull just as hard around a corner as on the straightaway. They can out pull a Holt any time on a corner."

Both tractors were steered by power and, by this time, both had brakes for each track. "It's not necessary to use the hand wheel at all, except on a straight road. On a crooked road, it is much easier for the driver, as he merely has to move a little lever back and forth in order to steer."

Rose found that the Best tractors could not turn quite so sharply as the Holts, probably owing both to Holt's individual track clutches and to Best's differential continuing to move the inside track. Mysteriously, Rose found out about a special Holt, one "for very marshy ground consisting of caterpillars only without a [front tiller] steering wheel. It is steered by throwing the caterpillars on each side into or out of gear. This machine is not cataloged, but it is about 40hp and sells for $3,000…."

"I understand that they turned out only a few of this type for this country but that this was the type which was made to order and sold to Germany for their guns long before the war."

Starr knew about that one. "Bill Turnbull was Holt's chief engineer at Peoria," Starr recalled, "at the time when the Holt plant began manfully to struggle to build its first Holt Caterpillars. Their sales department would take out and demonstrate a tractor on a stunt, like wading a river or climbing a bank. Turnbull finally got one built he thought was much better.

"Then he asked the sales department, 'Why in hell Sales could not sell one where it had a chance to do something?' Turnbull wanted the sales boys to demonstrate the tractor doing useful work.

"They did, and it worked and stayed sold. In my opinion," Starr declared, "Bill Turnbull had a major part in developing crawler-type tractors. He took the front wheel off. It was dropped because it was unnecessary.

"The first successful Caterpillar built at Peoria was the Holt 45, around 1914. Holt had one on exhibit at the Panama-Pacific Exhibition in San Francisco."

Starr settled himself and began again, with a laugh "That San Francisco Fair exhibit had a sidelight story I recall very well. The Holt 45 with no front wheel was rigged up to turn slowly in a circle on the floor. Dad Crook [E. I. Crook, Holt's Los Angeles distributor], who had been trained for the ministry, was in charge of the Holt exhibit and naturally he had to answer a lot of foolish questions. But he booby-trapped himself when he casually assured a visitor that it was a mechanical sheep herder.

"This fellow went away to spread the word among friends and he didn't see anything funny in being made to look foolish when his listeners finally convinced him that he had been sold a left-handed monkey wrench with an envelope-stretcher thrown in for good measure.

"He came back a few days later to check up, and was in a bitter, letter-writing mood after he discovered the turning machine was a tractor. Crook had to apologize."

Crook was a character, typical of the larger-than-life individuals who sold tractors in those days. Montgomery knew him well, and portrayed him vividly to Higgins: "Crook prided himself on knowing who was who in political and construction circles in Los Angeles. Dressed like a Hollywood cowboy, his boots and riding trousers—$50 to $80 creations—were cut by the best tailors and boot makers in Los Angelos. His working collection of sheriffs' badges covered three states and entitled him to rate among high officials anywhere."

1917 Best 75hp Tracklayer

The large fuel tank carried 75gal of distillate fuel although Darrach operates this Tracklayer only on gasoline. It easily pulled its six-disk 24in-diameter rotary plow to maximum depth.

1917 Best 75hp Tracklayer

Opposite page, farmers' families knew the tractor's whereabouts at night by looking for the flames from the twin exhaust stacks. The pale fires dance above the canopy, due to rich fuel mixture and nearly neutral timing.

1917 Best 75hp Tracklayer

Left, standard tracks were 2ft wide, overlapping pressed carbon-steel pieces.

1917 Best 75hp Tracklayer

Lower left, power steering turns the 2ft-wide, 4ft-tall front tiller wheel. It is operated by a chain-drive pump off the front pulley. A home-built oiler cared for the steering pump chain and the tiller-wheel gear.

1917 Best 75hp Tracklayer

Lower right, Dan Best's own 75hp four-cylinder engine could peak at 82hp at 500rpm. The 7.75x9.00in bore-and-stroke engine was designed with valves-in-head. With two forward speeds, the Tracklayer could reach nearly 2.5mph.

Chapter 5

War I: In Europe

Caterpillar Sales Overseas From Russia to Argentina ✦ *Chasing Pancho Villa With Caterpillar Tractors* ✦ *The Dawn of World War I* ✦ *"War" Holts* ✦ *Best Builds His Own Armored Prototypes* ✦ *"A War of Machinery"*

Caterpillar sales overseas—primarily the opening of South American markets—were initiated by Charles Parker Holt in late 1910. Uncle Benjamin, concerned about cashflow in the United States, thought it unwise. So, without family blessing, Charles Parker shipped a combine and crawler to Buenos Aires. Within a year, he'd sold nine, and by the end of 1911, 134 gas tractors, nearly half the company's entire tractor production, had been shipped through the Buenos Aires branch.

In the Spring of 1913, Benjamin and son William traveled to Kiev, Russia, to introduce their products to a vast new market. After one setback, the equipment performed perfectly, and a new continent was introduced to the Holt Caterpillar. The company had gathered its eight subsidiaries back under one umbrella of protective leadership, the Holt Manufacturing Company, and at about the same time hired L. W. Ellis to be its first advertising manager. One of Ellis' earliest accomplishments was to redesign the Caterpillar logo to reflect the movements of its namesake.

The war in Europe, from 1914 through 1918, affected Holt and Best dramatically—and differently. In late 1913, Holt—experienced with government contracts after the aqueduct project—began actively promoting his crawler's adaptability to military uses. But the War Department was not forward-looking. Even in early 1915 when Holt pointed out that the Austrian, British, French, and Russian governments had already bought more than 1,000 crawler tractors, US officials were unmoved.

In fact, the Austrian government had been so taken with Holt's machines that it tried to purchase the license to construct the tractors in Europe. Dr. Leo Steiner, a Hungarian farmer and engineer living in Austria, had purchased a Holt Caterpillar in 1910, and by 1912, he was the first European agent. He organized a series of tests with other manufacturers in which the tractors towed large howitzers over sand and through marshes. The Austrian War Department recognized the Caterpillar's value immediately, but the Germans in attendance were no more impressed than

the US government had been. However, negotiations with the Austrian government that had progressed until 1914, ended when the start of World War I arrested shipments of industrial materials from the United States. By that time, unfortunately, a number of the large Holts had been delivered for agricultural purposes to Austria. These appeared shortly after the outbreak of the war, operated by Germans plowing into Belgium.

At home, in frustration, Benjamin Holt offered to pay all the costs of demonstrations that the War Department selected—anywhere, any time. In early 1915, the US government consented, allowing two dates, one in May in Illinois at the Rock Island Arsenal, and a second in November in Oklahoma at Fort Sill. The military examiners were finally impressed, and a year later, the US Army Ordnance Department authorized the purchase of twenty-seven track-type tractors, to be manufactured at Pliny Holt's Peoria works.

Months before in 1916, when President Woodrow Wilson sent US Army General John Pershing into Mexico to find Pancho Villa and punish him for his deadly raid into New Mexico, Caterpillar tractors cut the roads and hauled the ammunition, food, fuel, and water 350 miles south into Mexico. "Blackjack" Pershing praised the Caterpillar crawlers in countless newspaper stories. And E. I. Crook, Holt's Los Angeles distributor, was not all bluff, bravado, and impersonation. He earned his reputation. "His chase of Pancho Villa under Pershing," Montgomery explained, "just before the United States went into the last war is a classic of war transportation over difficult terrain.... And he was in charge of the crawler tractors on this expedition."

Holt's farm tractors took on a new interpretation. The British, looking for a way to cross uneven fields muddied from rains and cratered by aerial bombardment, learned about Holt Caterpillars working on farms in Belgium. The machines were described as virtually unstoppable because of their long, steel tracks. Colonel E. D. Swinton of the British Army Engineering Corps described a series of specifications for a tracked war machine, and Great Britain's

1941 Caterpillar D7 Moving London Debris

Above, in January 1941, Londoners were surprised to see Caterpillar D7s with LaPlante-Choate R71 dozer blades being used for bomb debris clean up. Higgins collection

1919 Holt Midget

Opposite page, Holt's Midget was the company's first small tractor, designed specifically for the orchards and fruit tree groves. It was less than 4ft-6in tall. Steered by Holt's track brakes, steering clutches, and the tiller wheel, it was highly manueverable.

1919 Holt Midget

An expression "Knee high to a Caterpillar" comes to mind when Fred Heidrick, Sr's, Holt 9-18 Midget is parked in front of the Holt 60s and 75s. Few Midgets were produced; larger machines were needed for World War I.

Foster Company set out to build it. Among its other requirements, it had to be able to cross over an 8ft-wide trench and travel up to 4mph, and it had to be protected by steel armor nearly 1/2in thick.

The machine appeared. It was manufactured in Great Britain and battled in France despite its incomplete success—more than one-third of them broke down before getting to their first battle. Holt's Murray Baker (who had become a Holt Caterpillar Company vice-president in return for his help in acquiring the Colean plant in Peoria) seized a public relations moment, ignoring the fact that the Holt Company had nothing to do with the Foster machines. Interviewed by the *Washington Post*, Baker announced that: "We have sold about 1,000 Caterpillar tractors to the British government, but we had nothing to do with putting armor on them or placing machine guns….

"But some of our men at Aldershot, England, recently were notified that the British government intended to armor some of the tractors and use them for works other than the usual towing of guns."

To the rest of America, this meant that Holt's Caterpillar was "The Tank." Even when relaxation of government secrets allowed the truth to be known—that the British had merely modified the Tracklayer concept to produce a tank—many US citizens refused to accept the truth. Holt invented the tank. His reputation as industrial hero was sealed.

Holt's machines in Europe were armor plated, but not fully encased in armor. Still, the company's contribution was significant, beginning with retired engineer Henry Preble's candid comment on a parade field at San Francisco's Presidio. What he saw wasn't worth much, he muttered

Holt 18hp Midget

An early version of the Holt 18hp
Midget photographed on the dirt streets
of Stockton just outside the factory.
Higgins collection

aloud to everyone. A General standing nearby challenged his credentials, to which Preble outlined his employment with Benjamin Holt and stated that he had run the Aurora Engine Company and had participated in designing Holt's crawlers. The Army's problem, as Preble saw it, was slow-moving and awkwardly maneuvering machines. The Ordnance Department had already recognized these same short-comings in Holt's agricultural two-, five-, and ten-ton tractors. Almost immediately, Preble was out of retirement and back to work, employed by the Army at Holt in Stockton.

Gathering a team of young engineers, including Ed Wickersham, Ed Patterson, Charles Ball, Willis Yount, and Paul Weeks, Preble got permission from Baker in Peoria to start the project under the guise of being an 18hp agricultural tractor, to guarantee unrestricted access to men and raw materials from government-controlled stocks. Of course, it would not be an agricultural tractor and it would have much more than 18hp. Permission was granted.

Weeks drew the main frame. Steel was ordered. Preble and Wickersham visited the local Cadillac car agency and ordered a 75hp V-8 engine. Patterson called on the California National Guard to research light field artillery. He settled on the 75mm gun and the 105mm howitzer. Pattern makers Ball and Yount set to work creating a compound

transmission that would couple with the engine to drive the tracks individually for rapid turning. The top speed of the machines that Preble had seen at the Presidio was 6mph. The British and French had expressed the opinion that anything less than 15 to 18mph made the machine useless. Preble targeted 20mph. He began discretely spreading the word about the project in the Stockton and Peoria plants. He wanted to attract the best machinists, fabricators, and assemblers to work on it.

Informed of Preble's project, Pliny Holt began his own version of a 45hp crawler a week later. War was already declared, and competition between Peoria and Stockton was friendly but serious. Preble's prototype, complete with Week's extra-long tracks, was shipped back to Peoria for its first tests and then to Rock Island for the Army's "mud hole" tests.

Dig a hole. Fill it with water. Add dirt. Mix in six steel-shod mules. Stir thoroughly. Let other tractors attempt to go through it. And fail.

By the time Preble's 75hp Holt long-track got there, it was muck, not mud. But Week's long, wide tracks grasped and clawed and chewed their way out.

So much for the Army's mud. What about the European's speed? Patterson's crew had worried over that as

Ralph Easton and Best 30

Right, Ralph Easton, C. L. Best's most effective salesman, known for fighting with fists for any sale he couldn't make otherwise, looked ready to challenge the photographer to buy the rig or get out of the way. Higgins collection

1919 Holt Midget

Below, the Midget four-cylinder engine was cast en-bloc and produced 8hp at the drawbar using a Schebler 1.25in carburetor with an American Bosch magneto. This restored small Caterpillar is one of few known to exist, and is owned by Fred Heidrick, Sr.

1919 Holt Midget

Opposite page upper left, Holt and Best produced tractors in direct competition to each other often matching specifications and styles.

Austrian Army 120hp "War" Holt

Opposite page upper right, another of Holt's completion photographs. This 120hp "War" Holt wore the Army of Austria eagle on the fuel tank, prior to shipment from Stockton. Higgins collection

1917 Holt 120hp

Opposite page lower left, the 120 Holt used a six-cylinder version of the Aurora 7.50x8.00in bore-and-stroke gas engine. This is the only one known to exist.

well. Before shipping the prototype to Peoria, they took the crawler out to Sharp's Lane on the outskirts of Stockton one morning at dawn.

"We wanted to make sure," Patterson explained, "that the Army brass hats weren't going to give us California engineers the horse laugh. Between Sharp's Lane and French Camp, we got it up to 22mph, which we figured was good enough for the Army's specifications. We knew we had it after that first trial. And that was the speed the British said couldn't be done."

Holt shipped crawlers—Caterpillars—to the front and sent Weeks and Pliny Holt off to Washington to serve the War Department in the engineering and development of motorized warfare. Holt's ten-ton, beginning in 1917, was intended to tow the Army's 6in and 155mm guns and 8in and 240mm howitzers direct; the five-ton with 50hp and a top speed of 5mph was meant to transport the 4.7in gun and 155mm howitzer. And the Cadillac-engined two-and-one-half-ton was fitted with either 75mm guns or 105mm howitzers. It was put into war production in 1918.

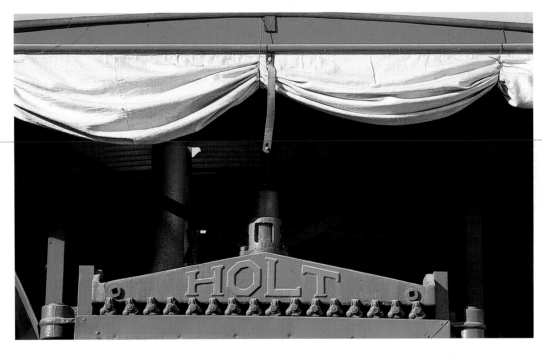

Following the war, General Pershing's Caliber Board recapped the lessons that it learned providing, operating, and repairing tractors in combat. What resulted was the Division Tractor, basically the two-and-one-half-ton fitted with a White sixteen-valve engine; The Corps tractor—for mid-size armor—was powered by a Sterling engine, weighed 8 1/2 tons and was capable of 10mph. And the Army tractor, designated in 1922, was more of a British tractor, weighing eighteen tons and fitted with a controlled differential to enable extremely tight turns.

A report authored by US Army Ordnance Captain L. A. Miller provided some insightful observations: "It may be concluded that a tractor built primarily for commercial purposes will not in all details be the absolutely ideal military vehicle. However, the comparative ease with which they may be produced in great quantities to meet the demands of war far outweighs any such shortcomings.

"The immediate requirements for track-type tractors in time of major emergency will be very great and it may not be possible that any commercial manufacturer will be able to meet them. For this reason, it is believed that in the early stages of such an emergency, use may be made of round-wheeled tractors."

Two other interesting vehicles were specified. One, a

1917 Holt 120hp

Above, front and side curtains protected the engine from wind-blown dust and scorching sun; the tin top protected the operator. This tractor was shipped to Marseilles but arrived there after the Armistice. This crawler now resides in Fred Heidrick, Sr's, collection.

French Soldiers and Holt 75

Above, five French soldiers pose with a Holt 75 tiller-wheel and artillery in the Ardennes Forest during World War I. Holt shipped 370 of the Caterpillars to the French government. Higgins collection

1917 Holt 120hp

Right, six big cylinders, thundering through the forests of Europe should have made any soldier question his future.

reconnaissance car to supplement the use of horses, advised fitting a Ford car with two extra axles and a fabric track. Independent brakes on the rear wheels assisted steering, but this system provided only short track life. The tracks were replaced with airplane tires fitted with tire chains. This performed exceedingly well until the temptation to add more seats and equipment met the limits of the engine and running gear. Overloading slowed it down too much.

The other was the "division motor gun carriage" meant for the 75mm gun. The Cadillac V-8 provided 15mph. "When it is desired to fire the gun," Captain Miller wrote, "outriggers or struts attached to the rear of the vehicle are quickly lowered to the ground and the brakes are set. The time required to prepare the mount for firing is not over two minutes...."

Its success led the Army Ordnance Division to dream: "One of the most alluring combinations for Army use is a vehicle adapted to run on rubber-tired wheels on the road and on a track, over and around the wheels, off the road. Several of such combinations have been tested...but no satisfactory vehicles have been discovered. Serious compromises in design are necessary."

Ben Holt and Col.

Ben Holt and British Col. E. D.
Swinton met after the end of the war
when Holt was given credit for
"inventing" the tank. The mini tank at
right was a scale model powered by a
motorcycle engine, mocked up for the
visit. Crawler at left was a Holt 75, the
US Army's World War I workhorse.
Higgins collection

Virtually all of Benjamin Holt's production was picked up by the US Army, while Best only shipped his tractors to the farms. Henry Montgomery, who was still Daniel Best's patent attorney, discovered some of the reasons it happened: "War broke out and the government wanted small tractors to pull 3in guns," Montgomery told Higgins years later. "The government filled Holt up with big tractor orders. They asked Best to send one to Rock Island for a trial. We built it—about six tons.

"The Best licked everything on tests at Rock Island."

Ralph Easton was there. Easton was a cowboy from the San Joaquin Valley who walked into the shops in San Leandro in 1909 and asked C. L. Best for a job. Because he was burly and walked with a definite swagger, he was given "the pig-iron treatment," stacking pig-iron ingots to be melted for castings for 9hr days at $1.25 a day. Easton stuck with it because, more than anything, he wanted to build and sell tractors and he knew that in order to learn, he had to work where they were made. After Best left Holt in 1910, Easton began to demonstrate Best's Tracklayers to potential customers. He retired from Caterpillar and went on to open Easton Tractor & Equipment in Alexandria, Louisiana, the Caterpillar agency for the middle of the state. He spoke with Higgins in 1931: "During the war, I was sent to Rock Island, Illinois, to inspect tractors and write reports. We had built in the tool room at the San Leandro plant a high-speed tractor. This machine was designed by Mr. Starr and Mr. Best, and was put out in less than six weeks time, and today I believe it excelled anything there at that time.

"We made 20mph with a full 3in gun, which included four ammunition carts, a limber, and a gun. It was a mystery to me why this machine was not adopted, as it showed the best report of anything that was tested at the arsenal at that time." Starr had understood that one deterrent to selecting Best's Tracklayers was Best's front tiller wheel. The British had experimented with a machine similarly configured, and had experienced problems with tractors hanging up over long spans such as wide trenches.

But Baker knew the real answer to Easton's question. He had a cousin in the War Department who had made the US Army his career. Baker confided a story, with some glee, to Higgins in 1952: "I dropped into the War Office at Washington, and I noticed the Best men waiting outside the door. My cousin asked me how he should handle them. I merely reminded him that he was a busy man. He should

Camouflaged Holt 10-Ton

Left, encased in armor, this Holt 10-Ton sat in front of the old Holt administration building. The Caterpillar logo appears to have been retouched later. Higgins collection

Best 30 in Army Trial

Below, a Best 30 with LaPlante Choate scoop loader dumps into a dumptruck. This photograph was shot at San Francisco's Presidio during crawler trials. Higgins collection

see them when he had the time. And I winked. My cousin kept those Best boys out there cooling their heels…and they never got anything beyond some tests at Rock Island."

All was fair in love and war, in the paneled offices in Washington, D. C., and in the grain fields of the West. The agricultural market was served as cleverly by C. L. Best whose dealer network numbered fifteen by 1918.

Frank Cornell was hired in 1910 to deliver C. L. Best tractors. "My job," he explained to Higgins, "was to go out and start an engine when it was sold to a farmer. I usually stayed with the engine for two weeks. The Best tractors at this stage had Buffalo motors. Best was turning out about one tractor a week."

Cornell remained with the new tractor and its owner until he felt comfortable with all the aspects of his purchase. But Cornell's other job was to operate the tractors for Best himself at the state fairs and other shows where Holt was likely to show up.

"Those tail-to-tail tractor pulling matches were always 'on the side'…. I recall one at West Sacramento in 1914 or 1915. Holt was there with their Seventy-Five which was the same size as C. L.'s was supposed to be," Cornell said. "I took a set of cylinders and bored them 1/8in bigger to give increased horsepower. No one else knew it. I was driving that Best and C. L. was on the outfit by my side as we gave our demonstration of deep plowing. I could feel the clutch begin to slip and smoke curling up from our Seventy-Five. The plow we were to pull had ten bottoms. 'Dare

we try it?' I muttered to C. L. We went in. 'Jesus Christ, Leo, we gotta stop before we burn out the clutch!' I said. 'Keep the S.O.B. going and never mind the clutch,' C. L. answered between clenched teeth. We finished that test plot, but there was no clutch left."

C. L. Best reminisced in a speech to his dealers twenty years later: "Those were the days when we went out from the factory with a tractor, started it to work, turned it over to the farmer as we took his check, and then raced like hell for the bank to get it cleared before he broke down and changed his mind."

However, Captain Miller had the last word, summarizing the applications of automotive equipment to the military: "There has been much speculation regarding the next war. The following is a quotation from Marshall Foch, which appeared in *The New York Times* during August 1926: 'It may come unexpectedly from anywhere and will be more terrible than the last. No one can see far ahead in these days, but of this we can be certain: Mechanical devices for winning battles will be the predominant factor. Brave men will still be essential to the proper handling of war machines, but it will be a war of machinery, rather than a war of flesh.'"

Holt Cadillac-Powered Prototype
Ben Holt's nephew, Mike Page, left, poses for a picture at the controls of Stockton 2.5-ton Cadillac 75hp-engined prototype. Top speed was 22mph. Higgins collection

Chapter 6

Fighting for Position

1919 Tractor Demonstration

Above, the "Best Boys" plan their

strategies before their demonstrations

at the tractor show at Walla Walla,

Washington, possibly in 1919.

Tractors include 30hp Tracklayer and

60 and 75hp Bests. Higgins collection.

1919 Best 60hp Tracklayer

Opposite page, a year and a half after

introduction, Best's Model 60 was

tested at the University of Nebraska.

It produced only 56.3hp at maximum

load. Still, the 17,500lb Tracklayer

pulled 11,000lb in low gear.

It was machine versus animal. "The thought at the Best factory was that we had to demonstrate our product to prove to a mule-and-horse farmer that he couldn't afford to stick with animal power any longer. Best was ready if the rancher was. And on the farmer demonstrations, I never failed." Frank Cornell explained. "Always came back with the money. Always left the tractor on the ranch where I demonstrated it."

In April 1915, as a reward for his sales success, Cornell was named manager of the Los Angeles territory, Best's newest branch. Together with his competition, Cornell organized the Southern California Tractor Dealers Association and it put on a four-day demonstration at Puente, a town in eastern L.A. county beginning September 19, 1915.

"Best, Holt, and Yuba [a track-layer tractor manufactured in Yuba City, California] were all there in a battle for crawler supremacy," Cornell reminisced. "We three paid no attention to the wheel tractors. We'd grown up, and we looked at such childish toys with disgust….

"I had the Best 75, the Best 30 'Muley' [a farmer's term likening tractors without tiller wheels to cows without horns], and the new 8–16. This one was aimed at the orchard [owner] and small rancher [and] was built to sell at $1,400. That little crawler was a pulling fool. It was aimed to match the Holt 9–18 'Midget', and Tom Luke, Holt's sales manager, had sold a lot of them.

"My serviceman, Charley Anderson, went out with this one and turned the world upside down with his demonstrations. We made such a show with this little Best that Holt canceled production of [its] Midgets to concentrate on war orders. At this Southern California show, Anderson and I worked all night every day of the show to keep that little Best demonstrating in top style every day. We would take out the rear end and overhaul it every night.

"C. L. was to make deliveries [the] first of 1916," Cornell continued. "I was paid $125 a month plus $50 on each 75, $75 on a 90, and $25 on each 8–16. I took fifty-two orders for that sweet little Best 8–16. Talk about feelin'

rich! That was me, all right, and I had it all spent when I got a wire from C. L. to cancel all the orders. The war had stopped production. Not enough steel."

Philip Rose had uncovered information about the 8–16 during his travels for General Motors in 1915. He learned that Best had spent $8,520 developing the tractor during 1914, but only a couple had been built. He postulated that it might fail since small tractors did not seem destined to do well on the large western ranches.

C. L. Best met with Henry Montgomery soon after the Puente demonstration. The more they watched Holt, the more certain they were that Holt was so busy with its government contracts that the company was not paying attention to the farmer.

"We'll have him," Best said to Montgomery.

G. B. Walker, the Caterpillar advertising manager, later clarified the differences between Best and Holt at this time: "While the manufacturing facilities of the Holt Company were practically commandeered by the US Ordnance Department, C. L. Best, realizing that agricultural activity must also proceed at top speed to ensure adequate food supplies, obtained assurance on that basis from Washington that he would be provided with adequate steel supplies that would permit him to continue to build tractors for farmers."

Best made it his goal to build tractors that didn't need to be rebuilt out on the farms. It was that kind of repair expense—in time and money—that harmed many of the wheeled tractor firms and that caught up with Holt after the war ended. Montgomery explained further: "War orders had swelled the Holt company. War tractors were tossed together with little inspection. The goal was to get them out [as] fast as possible. That was because the Army had plenty of soldier mechanics and parts to keep them going. But when sudden cancellation of war orders left lots of that kind of manufactured goods on the company's hands to sell to farmers, it was something else. The kind of tractors Best was now building were based [not] on war orders

1919 Best 60hp Tracklayer

Left, Best retained its separate cylinder castings. It used an Ensign Model G carburetor and ignition was accomplished by an American Bosch ZR41S magneto. Two speeds forward provided a top speed of 2.6mph.

1921 Best Model 30

Upper left, tested at University of Nebraska, the four-cylinder 4.75x6.50in bore-and-stroke engine produced 19.75hp on the drawbar and 30.4hp at the belt pulley at 810rpm. Its maximum tow was 4,343lb at just over 2mph.

1919 Best 60hp Tracklayer

Opposite page, Best introduced its 60hp Tracklayer in 1919 with its own 6.50x8.50in bore-and-stroke four-cylinder engine. It replaced the 75hp Tracklayer with front tiller wheel. Now it belongs to the Joseph Heidrick, Sr, collection.

but on the farmer as the whole market. And Best and the farmers taught each other."

Montgomery remembered Best telling his engineers to put a cap on the rear end of the tractor so that everything was easily accessible for service. "We talked over their production during those war months while the competition was getting the juicy war orders and we were making hay with the farmer. We set out to give the farmer a tractor that would be foolproof and keep going without trouble…. So when the new Best 30 and 60 came off the line, there was a pair of tractors that set new standards."

But Best had troubles, too.

After the war, Best retooled and broadened its line. This left C. L. with a $40,000 loss on the books for 1915. Oscar Starr remembered that things got interesting shortly after C. L. canceled Cornell's orders for fifty-two of the 8–16 tractors. Lack of funds restricted production to only two prototypes: "Rollin White [founder of White Sewing Machines and White Trucks] saw one of them at the Panama-Pacific Exposition in San Francisco in 1915 and bought it to take back to Cleveland sometime later. We always sold our experimental tractors in those days of short finances. White soon sent C. A. Hawkins, his White Sewing Machine Company sales manager, out to look over the Best and Holt plants with the idea that he might buy one of them and get into crawler tractor manufacture.

"Hawkins saw our Best exhibit…. The Best company was not a big financial success at this time," Starr explained, "so it was easy to buy control as several stockholder farmers were tickled to get out. Hawkins bought control of the wobbly Best Company by getting fifty-one percent [of the stock]. Best then asked for this 8–16 back, the one sold to White, but they insisted on keeping it. Out of their purchase and study of this tractor came the Cletrac."

Hawkins already had some tractor experience, albeit as an auto salesman, he explained to Higgins in 1951: "I knew Benjamin Holt and his brother Charley, who were automobile customers of mine at Stockton. Pliny Holt I knew better than either. My first interest in farm tractors was when Old Benjamin fired Pliny and he and myself

planned to start a company to build a tractor to sell for $500. 'The Ford of the tractor business,' Pliny called it."

"He had it all designed, and had tried to get his Uncles Benjamin and Charley to build it. Benjamin said he was crazy and fired him, so he came to me to get financed. Old Benjamin was pretty smart. He talked with me about it and argued that there was no place for so cheap and light a tractor. He claimed horses were better for small jobs—hay burners, he called them—because they fed on the farm and could do so many other things. Clarence White, the oldest of the White automobile family boys, had a pineapple plantation in Hawaii. He agreed to put some money into this company. Well, at that, Uncle Benjamin offered Pliny his job back at a raised salary, and Pliny took it."

Clarence White was an agricultural engineer who had once attempted to build a tractor—more a rotary plow—that failed in its tests. But as Hawkins and Clarence's brother Rollin watched Clarence's prototype fail, they saw a Yuba Ball Tread Tracklayer at work nearby in another field.

"Except for losing the large balls out of the ball race on which the track ran," Hawkins continued, "it was the best job we had seen. So we decided to build a small machine—without the balls. Thus, the Cletrac was born. We started in Euclid, Ohio, a small suburb of Cleveland, with $500,000. I took one-third; Rollin, one-third; [and]

Clarence and some other friends, one-third. Rollin was president; I was vice-president."

A factory was constructed, tractor plans were drawn, a prototype—basically Best's little 8–16—was photographed, and 1,000 dealers worldwide presold 12,000 tractors, taking a $50 deposit on each. Sales were based only on brochures and photographs, before a single one was built!

"The selling job I directed," Hawkins boasted, "as I had been the world's highest-paid sales manager with White Motors and White Sewing Machine—$175,000 a year."

Rollin White's own prototype was a disaster. Truck makers and sewing machine manufacturers did not understand tractor technology. Clarence's machine tore itself apart in the first two hours of testing. Angry over its performance and perceiving his whole experience as wasted time, Hawkins resigned, selling out to Rollin. (White did go on to redesign the tractor based more closely on Best's 8–16, and this version eventually became the first Cletrac tractor.)

According to Hawkins, Montgomery had begun surreptitiously arranging a merger of Best with Holt. Montgomery knew the strengths and shortcomings of both companies

and understood what putting the two companies together could mean. He worked with Best director A. S. Weaver to gather control of 60 percent of the C. L. Best Gas Traction Company stock and to hold it in escrow for Thomas F. Baxter, who had been hired as business manager of Holt's Stockton factory in 1913 and became its general manager two years later. A former investment banker from Boston, Baxter had been affiliated with Bond & Goodwin, a source of loan financing for Holt since 1910, and whose firm Charles Holt had come to know during his schooling and training years before in Boston. As a financier, Baxter had acquired large stockholdings in Holt's company, which he increased after joining the firm.

Best had been selling every tractor he could produce, but after 1915's losses, his investors were anxious to get out. They would accept whatever profit they could realize. Hawkins pounced. "Baxter, who had been ill, was unable to exercise the option in time," Hawkins told Higgins, "and I immediately spent $185,000 to buy the option. I took control of Best the next day. Baxter then telephoned me and offered $100,000 more than the option. I under-

1921 Best Model 30

Above, with its differential steering and track brakes, maneuvering the early Best Tracklayers was not easy.

1921 Best Model 30

Opposite page, Best's Model 30 in this configuration was called a "Muley," using farmers' terminology for a cow without horns, or for crawler tractors without front tiller wheels. This superb Muley is owned by Doug Veerkamp.

1921 Holt T-35

Top, the T-35 Caterpillar weighed just 4,040lb yet pulled 3,275lb. At 1000rpm the 4.00x5.50in four-cylinder engine produced 15.1hp on the drawbar. These models were originally known as the T-35. This one is part of the Joseph Heidrick, Sr, collection.

1922 Holt 10-Ton

Bottom, Holt's 10-Ton Caterpillar incorporated an operator's cockpit-mounted starting crank near the floor. A foot pedal engaged the chain. This restored crawler is part of the Joseph Heidrick, Sr, collection.

1922 Holt 10-Ton

Far right, also known as the T-11, this 9,400lb Caterpillar used Holt's own 4.75x6.00in four-cylinder engine. At 1050rpm, 33.3hp on the drawbar was produced and 5,558lb was pulled in first gear. The engine ran on kerosene or gasoline. The magneto is a German Bosch FU.4ARS54. An Ensign 2.25in carburetor was used.

stood his idea. We met soon afterward in New York and discussed a plan to put Best and Holt together in one strong company."

Starr apparently knew nothing of Montgomery's thwarted plan, but he disliked Hawkins: "I could see Hawkins was a promoter and not interested in real manufacturing…. Hawkins wanted to build tractors in the East at the Davis Sewing Machine Company in Dayton, Ohio, which he had gained control of. We designed a good, practical crawler, but Hawkins thought it was too heavy. C. L. sent me to Dayton to try to figure something out."

Montgomery had even more at stake. Realizing that he would be excluded from any Best-Holt merger orchestrated by Hawkins, he fought back. "Hawkins came in as the new president," he said, "after he had bought control from Charles Nelson, Best's brother-in-law, and some other farmers around Woodland. As the Best Company attorney, I had just delivered this patent coup to the Holt firm and at the same time I put the Best Company in a nice position as to working capital while making my own position in the Best firm look pretty good. About the first thing Hawkins did was to double his $15,000 salary. That immediately cut my salary, which was based on percentage of sales.

"Fred Grimsley, the new Best dealer at Stockton, met Hawkins and Best at their invitation for a duck dinner in

Colusa. Grimsley phoned me about Hawkins' plan to get rid of me. Fred had an unerring eye at spotting a four-flusher or phoney proposition, and he had the new Best president sized up before dinner was half over. In fact, this fresh young dealer from Stockton pulled C. L. off to one side as they got up from the table and warned him to get rid of Hawkins before he broke the company!"

With dealer backing and encouragement, Montgomery called a Board of Directors meeting, which Hawkins disdainfully referred to as a "rump session" and publicly vowed not to attend. He thought his three members of the seven-member Board of Directors would stay away as well.

"But there was one of the seven he didn't figure correctly," Montgomery remembered with satisfaction. "And he was on my side instead of Hawkins', and he appeared to give us a quorum and make the proceedings legal. We then voted the president out of power, made Best president, and proceeded to go along to prosperity.

"A few days later, Hawkins and his lawyer appeared at the plant and began circulating among the employees and talking against me and along the lines of what he would be doing shortly when he got back in control. Someone brought the word back to me, and I walked out to face Hawkins with the demand that he calm down.

"He made a pass and a swing or two at me before we tangled. He was such a huge man that my 150lb couldn't budge him off his feet for some little time. And by the time I toppled him over and he fell between some desks, I was swinging a right against his head and face, and he had to be helped up and taken out and washed up. He reported back to his lawyers that a gang of Best men had attacked and beaten him up!"

Still, Hawkins did some good. He spirited Bill Wagner away from the White Truck Company to set up Best's Tractor Service Department, the first in the business. Wagner adapted truck service to the tractor business, a difficult transition. When trucks broke down, they were probably parked somewhere accessible by paved road. Tractors, on the other hand, inevitably broke down in the mud, during a rain storm, at night, at the end of the field farthest from the deeply rutted dirt road.

Montgomery became more involved with the day-to-day operations at Best. He tagged along on product shows. He recalled going to Walla Walla to a demonstration in 1917 where Best had a 75 and a 40. The dealer had some trouble with the 40 and Monty went out with a serviceman to watch him work. It took two days to tear down the tractor to get ready to do the job on the rear-end bearings, then two hours to pour the bearings, and another two days to get it together again.

"That bearings pouring was something to see," Montgomery recalled. "That serviceman had to build a fire, heat up the babbit, and then pour it. That meant he had to carry a small blacksmith shop with him. That serviceman was no panty-waist short-hours-and-better-living lad."

Hawkins' other legacy was a fire he stoked in everyone's belly. Before he arrived, production at the Elmhurst factory was moving fast. In July 1913, Best's own four-cylinder engines were perfected and introduced. They replaced the six-cylinder Buffalo engines first fitted in the big 60hp round wheels from 1910 and the 75hp Tracklayers of 1912. At the same time, Holt closed up its operations in Daniel Best's old shops in San Leandro and moved all the machinery and its work back to Stockton. In August 1914, production of the Best Model 75 reached one per day; C. L. began to realize he needed more space.

In early 1916, a bond issue in San Leandro raised $20,000 to entice C. L. Best to return to his father's old shops. Within another few months, financing was arranged and C. L. moved his tractor company back to San Leandro. Through Harry Fair, a San Francisco bond broker and partner in Pierce, Fair & Company, a $400,000 loan was arranged. The land was reacquired, old buildings were razed, and modern shops were constructed. Fair had enough confidence in his new client that he even purchased Best stock for his own portfolio. Despite the cost to Best and the remaining shareholders to buy out Hawkins' interests, 1917 was a profitable year. Best and the Board of Directors declared an $80 cash dividend on every share of stock outstanding—stock that at the time bore a par value of $100.

By the spring of 1925, Best had forty-three dealers and nearly twice the business of five years earlier. Best tractors were well-designed, largely because of farmer input, and the new engines were reliable and well-regarded.

Best's seventeen-ton Model 75, costing $4,500, was introduced in 1912 and was manufactured through 1919. Just before the war, the company introduced the Model 30 and in 1915, it offered a six-ton Tracklayer 40, at $4,100.

Best's flexible tracks oscillated on spring-mounted trucks to accommodate small rocks and uneven ground without pitching the Tracklayer from side to side. His "rocker-joint" served the function of a track link pin without requiring lubricating grease that attracted and held dirt. This low-friction link system actually minimized track and link wear.

In 1916, Best introduced its biggest and smallest Tracklayers, the new 90hp twenty-ton machine and the ill-fated 8–16. The 90 stayed in production only through 1918, replaced by the legendary Best 60 Model 101. It was the first big Best without the front tiller wheel.

Holt was an aggressive marketer himself. Before the war, the US Army had remained convinced only of the mule's ability to pull supply trains, having had bad experiences with trucks. Holt concluded his letter-writing campaign successfully. He initially shipped his 75hp tiller-wheel Caterpillars to Europe. However, in 1917, he began to manufacture a new, 120hp six-cylinder. Holt expanded tremendously during the war, employing at one point 2,100 workers. The US Army ordered a total of 1,800 45hp tractors, 1,500 75hp tractors, and ninety of the big 120s. Holt's war output was substantial. Historian Wik counts a total of 5,072, with nearly 2,100 sold directly to the Allies.

Starr, at work in Dayton on a new, smaller tractor for Hawkins and Best, was pirated away to Peoria during this time. "Pliny Holt had got into the war picture back in 1915 or 1916," he recalled. "He came over to Dayton and told me they were in a big jam at Peoria trying to fill the British and French Governments' war orders for Caterpillars. 'I'm ambitious! Make it enough money and I'll come over and help out,' I told Pliny. So Pliny did and said, 'Come on over,' and I was in Peoria in 1917. I got the War Holt 75s into production in two versions, one for the United States and one for the British. I was getting production up to two or three a day. Then the US government had designed two more special war tractors, the T-16 and the T-35, I believe. Those I was to put into production also. The T-16 never got into production."

Holt's lineup suffered from the wartime success of capacity production. There was no spare time to pursue domestic sales, no spare personnel to service it or to conceive of and develop new tractors. Holt produced only a limited line of products—heavy, powerful tractors—due to the changes required by US government specifications that yielded machines ill-suited to agriculture. Holt came out of four years of heavy production with large inventories, tractors that could not be easily adapted to farming, and poor cashflow. And peace treaties canceled all the wartime contracts. Tractors completed, ready for shipment, were not going to be paid for or even accepted.

By 1920, the United States was entrenched in a nationwide economic depression. High wartime production levels overtook reduced postwar demands in everything from food to cloth to machinery. Over-production caught up with Holt from both sides. The American farmer who had needed machinery to meet wartime food demands lost his markets once peace came. Worse yet for Holt, the government was now oversupplied with tractors. Many were sold cheaply to state highway departments. But many more began to flood into the market as inexpensive "war-surplus" Holt crawlers.

When Benjamin Holt died in December 1920, he left a company reeling from its wartime successes—but it was also over-extended and scrambling to survive. Frequently, large corporations finance daily operations on short-term credit. The most influential of its lending institutions often acquires at least one seat on the Board of Directors—Baxter was invited to join the Holt Board of Directors in July 1917—which ensures the lender's proximity to all fiscal decisions. As the credit increases, so does the influence, often resulting in a former officer of the lending institution becoming the chief officer of the borrower's entire corporation. Such was the case here: Holt's Stockton general manager Thomas Baxter, the former Boston banker, assumed Benjamin Holt's title as president.

Baxter ruled Holt with an iron hand, running the business with an eye to financial responsibility. He cut the large tractors—the 120hp crawlers—from the lineup, and hurriedly attempted to develop and introduce smaller models more suited to agricultural purposes. He learned of a $1 billion federal highway building fund and began directing company advertising toward road contractors.

Thus, as Baxter spent money to revise Holt's line, the corporate debt increased further. The result was a two-edged sword that with one swath improved the machines while with the other required full-capacity production to pay its way.

An outside consultant recommended in 1923 that Holt produce smaller tractors and cut its Model 75. Production should be consolidated in Peoria, Baxter was advised, because shippers charged extra to get materials to Stockton. But the War Department had shipped the molds for Holt's smaller engines to another plant for wartime assembly. So even after the armistice in November 1918, it took years for them to be returned. With only about 60 percent of the total shop floor space—in Stockton and Peoria combined—used, Holt's debt was continuing to rise. Without economic recovery or a miracle, Holt was on unstable footing.

The C. L. Best Gas Traction Company was in little better shape. C. L. Best had fought Holt's marketing trick-for-trick before the war. Best offered large trade-in allowances and favorable financing. Both makers knew that a plentiful new customer base existed among horse-and-mule farmers. These were men who had lost helpers, workers, or family members in the war, and they needed machines. Short-handed, they could no longer manage a dozen or more draft animals.

But how should the tractor makers handle those farmers? This question would continue to be difficult to answer for another decade.

Starting procedure for Holt Ten-Ton Tractor

1. Move the master clutch hand lever to the "out" position.
2. Move the gear shift into the "neutral" position.
3. Move the spark lever from the "full retard" position to about one-eighth advanced. Note: All ten-ton tractors have a circuit breaker grounding switch. The magneto is grounded and the engine is stopped by pulling the spark lever to the "full retard" position. To start the engine, the spark lever should be advanced only enough to open the switch. Never crank the engine on advanced spark.
4. Open the throttle about one-quarter and do not change this setting until the engine has run long enough to warm up.
5. Trip the impulse starter by pressing down on the back of the ratchet catch lock, releasing the ratchet catch and bringing the impulse starter into operation.
6. Prime the cylinders if the engine is cold or has not been operated in a long time. Open the priming cups by pulling the priming cup gang lever toward the driver and, using a squirt can, put three or four drops of gasoline in each cup. Close the priming cups. Do not overprime.
7. Open the compression release cocks.
8. Crank the engine using the hand starter. To get the best results from the hand starter, turn the crank until the starter gear meshes with the teeth on the rim of the flywheel. Pull up slowly on the hand starter crank until you're on a compression stroke, then give a quick pull or flip past center.
Note: The hand crank engine starter is a modification of the Bendix drive principle in general use on automobiles. The

turning movement of the starting crank is imparted to a sprocket and thence by a roller chain to a similar sprocket mounted on a shaft, carrying the starter gear. The sprockets are supported in a bracket bolted onto the main frame of the tractor slightly to the rear and to the left of the engine flywheel. A foot button mounted on the bracket when depressed causes the starter gear to rotate and ensures it meshes with the teeth in the flywheel.

Caution: Do not keep your foot on the starter button after engaging a gear. The pin prevents the starter gear from backing out of the teeth in the flywheel when the engine starts, and the operator will be injured if the engine starts.

9. Once the engine starts, advance the spark. Always keep the spark as fully advanced as possible without having a "spark knock" in the engine. Experience will indicate the proper position.
10. Adjust the engine speed by placing the hand throttle lever in such a position that the engine will idle at low speed.
11. Engage the gear speed desired by placing the gear shift lever in the slot designating the speed to be used. Speed up the engine by slowly advancing the hand throttle lever.
12. Engage the master clutch slowly until all slack is taken up between the engine and the load. Then engage the clutch firmly.
13. To steer the tractor, use the steering clutch hand levers operating the steering clutch located on either side of the transmission unit. Release the steering clutch on the side of the tractor toward which the turn is to be made, and apply the foot brake on the released clutch.

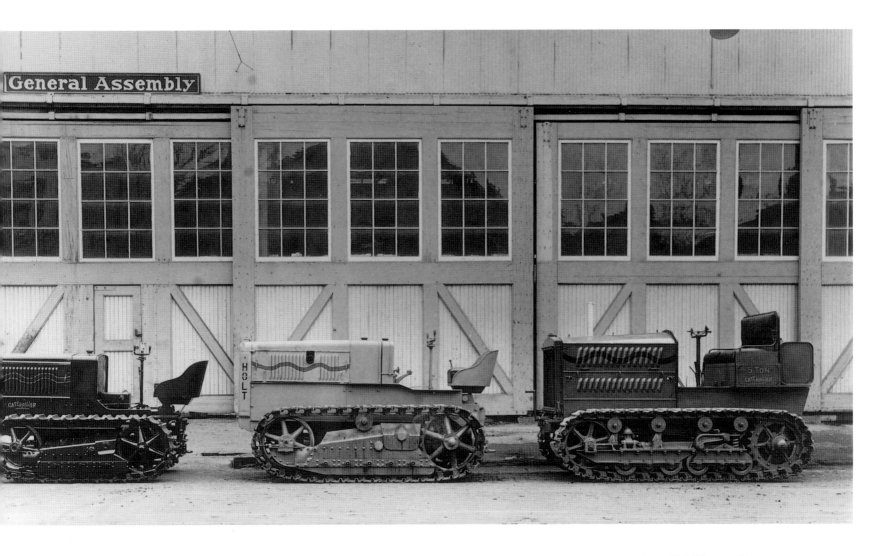

General Assembly

Holt Wartime Lineup

Above, Holt's war lineup: T-35, T-29, and 5-Ton parked outside of the general assembly shops in Stockton. Higgins collection

Holt 5-Ton

Left, a war surplus armored 5-Ton grades a road in Arkansas. This was one of many decommissioned Holt Caterpillars from the US Army and Marines that was issued to various states for their highway departments. Higgins collection

Chapter 7

Merger by Any Other Name

A New Name For New Times in 1920: C. L. Best Gas Tractor Company ✦ *Lawsuits Drag Down Both Firms* ✦ *Merger Talks* ✦ *The Caterpillar Tractor Company is Formed in 1925* ✦ *Sales Double, Profits Triple*

1929 Caterpillar Model 60

Above, in low gear, Caterpillar's Model 60 was capable of 12,360lb of draw. Doug Veerkamp's restored 60 performs as well as it looks in the fields near Placerville, California.

1929 Caterpillar Model 60

Opposite page, the Model 60 maneuvered with track brakes and clutches. In third gear at 650rpm, the 20,000lb Model 60s could pull 6,240lb while burning 7.8gal of gasoline per hour.

Reacquiring C. A. Hawkins' stock had contributed to Best's financial straits. Its primary financial resource was a prominent bond brokerage house in San Francisco called Pierce, Fair & Company. Harry N. Fair and C. L. Best had worked together frequently, securing and funding short-term loans for Best's business. Fair had arranged the $400,000 loan for C. L. to reacquire his father's shops in San Leandro.

Best and Fair had a good rapport. Even more important, Fair was also a friend of Raymond C. Force, who had become Best's attorney after Hawkins was forced out and Montgomery went to work for Holt. Fair, Best, and Force met through their work with Victory Bond Drives during the war. Fair became a significant Best stockholder, and both he and Force were offered a seat on Best's Board of Directors in June 1920.

One year earlier, in July 1919, as Best introduced his Model 60, Force and Fair assisted C. L. in expanding his company. Force filed an amendment to the Articles of Incorporation to increase capital stock to $10 million and bonded indebtedness to $300,000. Within the next year, the company changed its name to the C. L. Best Gas Tractor Company and increased indebtedness to $750,000 (partly to pay off Hawkins). One further increase took place in May 1923, authorizing a total $1 million of bonded indebtedness to finance still further growth.

But with costs of the technology and expansion, it remained difficult for C. L. Best to pay his bills and his employees.

Holt also found day-to-day financing difficult. Meeting payroll required the timely sale of a tractor. At the time, Holt Manufacturing Company's charter allowed $6 million in capital stock since June 1918.

Legal costs of the suits and counter-suits between Best and Holt from 1907 to 1918 totaled more than $750,000. This did not include the costs of damages, settlements, and patent purchases that each incurred. Total costs were likely to have been more than $1,500,000.

Holt historian Reynold Wik put together much of the on-stage and in-the-wings activities that followed Benjamin Holt's sudden death in December 1920.

Thomas Baxter flexed his financial muscle. He threw the clout of his banking and bond house behind a threat to simply let Holt Manufacturing go under if he were not named president. Holt's heirs and successors preferred Murray Baker because he knew more about the tractor business and was more personable. But Holt's long-time corporate counsel, Charles Neumiller, advised the Board of Directors that Baxter's clout—and threat—were real. They had little choice but to accept Baxter if they wanted to have a Board of Directors on which to serve.

Baxter's authority was total. After several years of suffering almost tyrannical austerity, Baker and several other key stockholders surreptitiously approached Harry Fair. Baker's idea was to shift the Board of Directors' favor to Pierce, Fair & Company for principal financing of Holt's indebtedness. But with four years of experience on Best's Board of Directors, Fair had come to know the tractor business intimately. As the handsome, dapper San Francisco financier charmed members of the Holt Board of Directors, he became aware of Holt's business conditions. He recognized that neither Holt nor Best had a commanding lead over the other. Each operation competed directly with the other in every major commercial market in the world. They duplicated everything from sales branches and service staffs to the brochures, service orders, and sales invoice paper forms necessary to their support.

Fair grew concerned for his own investments. In the shrinking economy, could Best repay its loans? With neither company dominant, could both fail? Without consulting C. L. Best beforehand, he went back to Baker and, presumably, to Pliny Holt as well.

If they were to join together with Best, Fair proposed, the savings to each company would be enormous. Together, they would command the leading position in crawler tractor sales worldwide. There would be no difficulty in finding new investors if such were needed. But debt could

be restructured. Existing stockholders would be well rewarded, receiving shares in a strong new company that could take advantage of the skills, technologies, reputations, and customer loyalties of the two shaky independents.

Fair put it together—in two steps.

Historian Reynold Wik quoted the first step: A telegraphed press release dated March 2, 1925, was issued from Peoria. In it, Baker announced Baxter's resignation and Holt corporate counsel Charles Neumiller's promotion to company president. "The control of the Holt Manufacturing Company, which for the last thirty years has rested in the Holt family and more recently in the Benjamin Holt Corporation has passed to a group consisting of Pierce, Fair & Company of San Francisco and associates."

The associates included, of course, Holt family members and Baker.

On April 15, 1925, the other shoe dropped.

Allen Chickering of the law firm of Chickering & Gregory in San Francisco filed with the office of Secretary of State of California document number 113767, the Articles of Incorporation of Caterpillar Tractor Company. This simple five-page document established the new company. Its

purposes were, among others: "To manufacture, produce, buy, sell, import, export, or otherwise acquire, dispose of, or deal in tractors, harvesters, machinery, agricultural implements, and vehicles of every kind and character."

Capital stock in the new corporation was set at $12,500,000, divided into 500,000 shares with a par value of $25 each. Its Board of Directors, each granted one single share of stock, consisted of nine names that few people familiar with Best or Holt tractor history would recognize.

On May 4, Chickering filed papers authorizing a $5 million bonded indebtedness. That same day, The Holt Manufacturing Company held a special stockholders meeting to notify its investors of its intent to dissolve. The C. L. Best Gas Tractor Company shareholders met the next day for the same purpose. And within two months, the Superior Court of the State of California ordered voluntary dissolution of the two corporations.

At the close of business June 23, 1925, The Holt Manufacturing Company stated in newspaper notices that it had 171,683 shares of stock outstanding, with a par value of $4,292,075. The C. L. Best Gas Tractor Company published its outstanding stock at 88,308 shares with a par val-

ue of $2,207,700. On paper, Best was worth roughly half the value of Holt. On August 28, Caterpillar Tractor Company moved its office and principal business from Number 1232, Merchants Exchange Building, San Francisco—the same building with Chickering's law office—to 700 Davis Street, San Leandro, the most recent home of C. L. Best Gas Tractor Company.

In a series of moves that today might raise legal eyebrows, Harry Fair took care of himself. But he clearly took good care of his clients as well, in the order of their importance and their contribution to the new corporation. When the dust settled, the reorganizing of Best and Holt was not a merger but was more accurately, as Reynold Wik characterized it, a "consolidation."

The articles of incorporation allowed for the creation of no new stock. Existing Best and Holt shares were exchanged for the same number of Caterpillar shares. Fair represented Best shareholders at the same time that he was attempting to secure Pierce, Fair & Company's services for Best's competitor. These events led him to act in his own interests. Those interests—in retrospect—seemed to be in some conflict with C. L. Best's interests: C. L. had broken a legal sales agreement with Holt fifteen years earlier when he returned to business producing tractors in direct violation of the terms of the agreement. Best obviously wanted no part of the Holts in 1910. So it seems only fair to conclude that Fair, while reconstructing Caterpillar Company, sought to benefit those who had benefitted him—even if they had done so unwittingly. After all, C. L. had publicly stated—in the years before and after 1925—that he "thought the world of Harry Fair." In the papers filed on the June 23, 1925, C. L. Best was listed as chairman of the Board of Directors and Raymond C. Force was designated as president of the new corporation. Percy Ehrenfeldt, former secretary of Holt, was retained as secretary of the new company.

But this was only part of the story.

Henry H. Howard joined Caterpillar as a twenty-two-year-old economics graduate in May 1926. He was first assigned to the Parts Department to learn the machines and the company. By the time he retired in 1961, he had served as vice-president of sales for nearly ten years. Soon after his arrival, Howard was deemed too well-educated for Parts and was transferred to the Export Department to work under Charles Parker Holt—who told Howard all about the late spring of 1925.

"Parker had been treasurer of Holt Manufacturing," Howard explained recently at home in Solvang, California. "Immediately after the merger, Parker was told there was no place for him in Caterpillar. You know, the merger was a bitter affair, rough. Bests came in, and they fired practically everybody. They just didn't want any piece of the Holt boys around there—Benjamin's boys, that is: Bill, Al, Dean, and Ed. So that rule, that no family members of directors could work at Caterpillar, came into existence because of the Holt boys. But Pliny and Murray Baker were safe. They were on the Board of Directors and anyway, they needed somebody to run the Peoria operation. And Pliny Holt saved these two engineers, Harmon Eberhard and Willis Yount. Parker said he'd work for Caterpillar if he had to sweep the floors. So they said, 'Give Parker Export, let him play with it.'"

B. Claude Heacock had become a Best Board member in 1920. When Caterpillar relocated all its offices to Peoria, Force was unwilling to leave California and Heacock was named president. Heacock was at Stockton from the first days of the new company. Years later, he related to Howard his own experiences from that period: "I remember Heacock telling me about going into a room with fifty people in it and telling them all to put their things up and walk out and get a two weeks paycheck. And he said they burned the Holt records at Stockton."

Howard paused to let the story sink in. "They burned all the Holt records and they stoked the furnaces so that ashes—unburned letters—scattered all over town."

Within eighteen months of the consolidation, the real organizational and operational power was in place and on file with the state. Force was still president and C. L. Best was still chairman of the Board. Heacock and Starr were moved over from Best, joined on the Board by Pliny Holt, Baker, Fair, and Chickering. It was perhaps Fair's way of repaying Pliny and Baker for their assistance from the beginning.

Even before the Board maneuvers were complete, the shortcomings in the product line were consolidated. Renamed Caterpillars, Best's 30hp and 60hp Tracklayers survived. Best's forty-three US dealers were merged with Holt's seven exporters. Total sales jumped 70 percent up—something Fair anticipated—even as Ford and International Harvester entered price wars lethal to all of their wheeled-tractor competitors. But Caterpillar remained almost neutral in that war. Wheeled tractors simply did not infringe on crawler sales—something else Fair had anticipated.

Best's tractors were more advanced. The somewhat more leisurely pace of agricultural sales during the war, coupled with a sales force dedicated to understanding—and filling—the farmer's needs, permitted the continued development and evolution of Best's line.

Equally valuable, Holt brought in its name recognition and worldwide reputation as well as its complete control of all pertinent patents. Holt's plant facilities were six times the size and its sales revenues were still twice as large as Best's immediately before the consolidation. And Holt brought its two-, five-, and ten-ton tractors. Almost immediately, however, the five- and ten-ton models were discontinued because they were determined to be somewhat outdated and too costly to produce and required more parts for assembly than the Bests.

In late 1925, the new Caterpillar Company published prices for its product line: The Model 60 sold for $6,050; the Model 30, $3,665; and the two-ton, $1,975.

The consolidation of the two companies proved its value over the next few years. It not only benefitted Caterpillar shareholders, but sales more than doubled between 1926 and 1929, from $21 to $52 million, and profits nearly tripled, from $4.3 to $12.4 million. More efficient manufacture and use of facilities substantially reduced prices on the big tractors. The price of the Model 60 was cut to $4,300, and the Model 30 was relisted at $2,475—both reductions of nearly one-third. Fair had lived up to his personal credo for the goal of a successful business: "In time of decision, the responsibility of the company [is] to [the] shareholder, customer, and employee."

Some problems were not solved by the consolidation of Best and Holt. In 1909, when there were only nine tractor companies in the United States with total production of barely 2,000 machines, farm work still got done. It merely required more than 24 million horses and mules. In 1925, there were fifty-eight manufacturers, though this was down from the peak of 186 in 1921. These makers produced slightly more than 164,000 tractors. Still, there were 22,558,000 mules and horses left on farms. Every dozen or two dozen horses and mules represented a potential tractor buyer…if there was some benefit to trading away paid-for draft animals that ate off the farm's production.

Farmers were quite happy to get rid of their mules because with them went the mule skinners, the hired hands who got drunk on Sundays and missed work on Mondays. Starr remembered with a sense of irony what happened when the mule skinners met the Caterpillar men: "They were better at following instructions on tractor service than the factory men we sent out from the shops. These mule skinners made the best Caterpillar skinners after you taught them how to care for the tractor."

And, as Starr recalled, Caterpillar's factory men learned a trick or two from the mule skinners: "It was a common practice on cold mornings to start the tractor with a mule. A rope was put around the flywheel. A mule was hitched onto the loose end and the mule was slapped on the ass to get him out of there with a lunge that started the gas engine on the tractor."

So, what was a horse or a mule worth in trade? It was a question that even Fair's wizardry with numbers couldn't settle clearly. Higgins wrote a story for Caterpillar years after the problem of animal trades ceased to exist. He called the situation "The Big Un-Hitch."

"From the earliest days of big ranching and freighting in the Stockton area," Higgins wrote, "the local operators had bragged about having 'more horses in front of a single driver and more wagons behind him than anywhere else in the world.' Six- and eight-horse plows and wagons were almost standard on every ranch, and thirty-two-mule teams pulling combines were the usual things, with an many as forty animals used on the hilly ranches with big cuts and heavy crops. Dealers like Fred Grimsley and Frank Cornell carried horse buyers with them to help handle the deals that took the mules and horses in exchange as down payments on tractors and combines."

In a memo dated September 16, 1927, Oscar Perrine, head of the Caterpillar Service Department, dispatched a request for an unusual bit of research for the company's sales staff. He needed to know how many mules or horses were usually shipped in a railroad stock car and what the rates per car were.

His resulting memo informed the sales staff that twenty-six to twenty-eight animals could be transported from Fresno to Los Angeles for $91.50, to Phoenix for $151, or to Seattle for $324.

Two days later, Perrine wrote to I. E. Jones, vice-president in charge of Western sales: "The mule problem grows. Dan Beatie and Bill Grimsley say they can sell about eight 60s if they can dispose of enough mules. They say they can get a lot of good ones—young, sound, heavy—but will have to allow from $150 to $175 for them, and can't resell for over $100 and then only in small lots."

A day later, S. V. Chown in the Sales Department wrote Perrine: "Subject: Mules eat hay. Mr. P. Hoare of Hayward has 120 mules, and said there would be no market until spring, as it will soon begin to rain and that will mean feeding the mules through the winter. I talked to one of the men at Miller & Lux's regarding some pasture, and he will let me know on Tuesday whether they could take them, and the price per month per mule."

Two days later on September 23, Jones wrote Perrine again: "My dear Mule Expert: "I have your long, mulish letter, which I have read very carefully, and in some ways I believe you have the wrong slant. We do not intend to go into the mule business...."

Grimsley, Cornell, and others learned hard lessons, paying too high a price for "hay burners." At such prices, they couldn't resell them quickly enough and ended up los-

ing more in pasturing and feeding their "ass-ets." Perrine eventually conducted a survey to determine the number of horses and mules still in farmer hands where Caterpillars might replace them. As a marketing tool, Perrine finally suggested that Caterpillar might need to build a new plant. This one would specialize, he said with a straight face, "in the slaughter and canning of horse and mule meat for export in order to increase tractor sales to farmers."

In the meanwhile, the gasoline-powered four-cylinder engines, as the company's mainstay, were being shaken up just as thoroughly as the entire Caterpillar product line had been. In Germany, which had given birth to the four-cycle Otto gasoline engine, other engineers were developing yet another new four-cycle engine. This one made a new sound. It used a new fuel. And it produced a new, more efficient, less-expensive power than gasoline, steam, or animals had done before.

1926 Caterpillar Model 60

After the Best-Holt consolidation, mainly Best tractors survived. Continually improved by farmer input, the Best 30 and 60 also used fewer parts in their manufacture than the Holt 5-ton and 10-ton models.

Chapter 8

Sound and Fury

*The Development of the Diesel Engine ✦ Diesel Experiments
and Conversions ✦ Building the First Caterpillar Diesels ✦
"An Exciting Time to be Working at Caterpillar"*

The gasoline-engined Best 60 that appeared in 1919 and was adopted as a full-fledged Caterpillar in 1925 succumbed in 1931 to technological evolution. Its passing was not swift. It did not go without a fight.

A new engine, converted from gasoline, was sent out into practical field use on September 14, 1931. A Model 60 Tractor, designated the 1C series, changed the sound and style of Caterpillars for ever. The prototype, tractor no. 1C1, stayed with Caterpillar in the San Joaquin Valley for testing and development. The four-cylinder 6.125x9.25in engine displaced 1090ci. In all, 157 of the new series of Diesel 60 were produced.

The engine's German inventor, Rudolf Diesel, had planned to call it the Delta engine, or possibly "The Excelsior." On paper, he referred to it as the "Rational Heat Engine on the Diesel Patent." But while he was agonizing over its name and fretting over so many other problems in early October 1895, his wife said to him, "Just call it a Diesel engine."

Diesel had the idea for his engine while still a teenager. For him, higher education included years at the School of Industry in London and a degree from Munich's Polytechnikum before he was twenty years old. Exposed to the theories and engines of Thomas Newcomen, James Watt, and Nikolaus Otto, Diesel challenged himself to invent a heat engine more powerful and more efficient than theirs. By 1890, he had revised his idea and began to conceive of a high-pressure air engine—the air heated quite hot by its extreme compression—into which a fine mist of fuel would be injected at its most compressed stage. The resulting explosion would force the piston back down the cylinder. His paper on this theory, published in 1893, earned him his first German patent.

Diesel's engine operated on the basis of Otto's four-cycle gasoline engine. But Otto's second stroke, compression of fuel and air mixture just before spark, became Diesel's compression stroke with plain air alone, and his engine achieved six to eight times more compression than Otto's. This heated the air at the top of the stroke so much that all

he needed to do was introduce a volatile fuel mixture; no spark was necessary. The cylinder's contents would explode through the third stroke, pushing the piston down as the combustion expanded the mixture in the cylinder, with exhaust following on the fourth stroke, just the same as Otto's engine. Yet it required years of experiments to make it work.

At the same time, Adolphus Busch, the St. Louis, Missouri, beer brewer, came to Munich to see Diesel. After thoroughly examining the engine and getting the opinions of other theoretical scholars and practical engineers, Busch watched some experiments. Then, in October 1897, he signed a contract with Diesel to produce Diesel engines in the United States. Diesel asked Busch for a license fee of $1 million—and Busch never blinked! Busch began building the first Diesels in the United States in 1898.

The world had come to understand what Diesel knew: His engine used as little as one-third the amount of fuel needed by the Otto gasoline engine to produce comparable work. A group of American engineers came to Germany in early 1913 to invite Diesel to appear with his engine at the San Francisco World's Fair in 1915. He would sail to the United States on a diesel-powered ship.

Unfortunately, Diesel was psychologically troubled from the first by his failures and his depression did not end when he became successful. In fact, following his undisputable fame and triumphs (including several honorary degrees), he was plagued even more by the jealousy and treachery of others who tried to steal or revile his invention. And so on September 29, 1913, sailing on the North Sea from Hamburg, Germany, to Ipswich, England, to supervise the opening of his engine factory there, Diesel simply slipped over the side of the ship late in the night. His body was found and his identification was confirmed days later.

It fell to Robert Bosch—maker of magneto sparking devices for airplanes, automobiles, trucks, and tractors—to substitute Diesel's high-air-pressure fuel injection system with

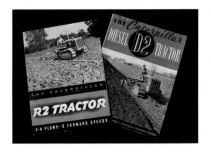

R2 and D2 Brochures

1931 Caterpillar Model 60 Diesel

Opposite page, this Model 60 was the the 12th diesel Caterpillar sold, delivered to Mark Weatherford at Fairview Ranch in Arlington, Oregon. In 1935, it was sold to Allen Anderson's family, farming near Ione, Oregon, where it has remained since then.

1931 Caterpillar Model 60 Diesel

Above, Nicknamed "Old Tusko" after an elephant that lived at the Portland zoo.

1931 Caterpillar Model 60 Diesel

Right, Caterpillar used a two-cylinder gasoline pony engine to start the diesel. It directed exhaust back toward the diesel fuel injectors and cylinder walls. Engaging its small power take-off cranked over the much-higher compression diesel engine.

1931 Caterpillar Model 60 Diesel

Left, the diesel engine displaced 6.125x9.25in and produced 54 drawbar and 77.1 brake horsepower at 700rpm.

1931 Caterpillar Model 60 Diesel

Below, this 25,860lb diesel powerhouse pulled 11,991lb in low gear.

hydraulic injection of the mixture into the cylinders. Bosch's work began shortly after the November 1918 Armistice. A number of engineers and experimenters had begun working on a reliable fuel feeding system. By late 1922, Bosch was seriously involved, and for the next four years, he and his engineers attempted to devise methods of blasting—twenty times a second—a microscopic drop of fuel into a Diesel combustion chamber against very high back pressure.

By 1927, trucks from Benz, Daimler, and M.A.N. participated in an extended driving test. Bosch's pump on Diesel's engine was reliable enough that three more Benz Diesel trucks began making shuttle runs among various Bosch factories in Europe. Another one was shipped to New York in late 1927 for deliveries in the East. Bosch delivered its one-thousandth Diesel engine fuel-injection pump before 1928. It was ready to gear up for the mass production that it believed the world's industry would demand.

The Diesel engine made it to San Francisco for the 1915 Panama-Pacific Exposition. Displayed by the Danish maker, B&W, the engine operated a generator in the Machinery Building, not far from the displays of Best and Holt gasoline-engined tractors. While his brother-in-law, Charles Manning, ran the Best display, C. L. Best and Oscar Starr came frequently to the city to see, study, and ask questions about the new engine. Its economy of operation convinced both men that they had to get some version of it into a tractor someday.

Shortly after Busch had been licensed to produce Diesel engines in St. Louis, another American, George A. Dow, a pump manufacturer in Alameda, California, had visited Diesel during his early trips to Ipswich in 1911 and obtained production rights. Dow received his license from the British makers in Ipswich.

In the years between the 1915 Exposition and the Best-Holt consolidation, Best and Starr maintained close contact

1931 Caterpillar Model 60 Diesel

The diesel's greatest performance was its

economy: 13.87hp-hours per gallon of fuel.

with Dow. And in late 1925, when the new Caterpillar chairman got some breathing room, he saw Dow again.

"Leo Best was an old schoolmate of mine," Dow told Hal Higgins years later. "I recalled seeing him at the Sequoia Club one day, and he asked me where he could get a high-grade Diesel engineer. He had decided to go into Diesel tractor building.

"I said he could have my engineer, as I was ready to quit. That man was [Art] Rosen, who I got from the University of California."

Ironically, Rosen, a young mechanical engineer with an

acquired background in marine uses for Diesel power, had begun writing to Pliny Holt as early as July 1923. Rosen hoped to interest Holt Manufacturing in applying the Diesel engine to its tractors. Pliny Holt introduced the idea to the directors, and correspondence continued throughout the next year. Willis Yount, who worked for Harmon Eberhard, head of Holt's Engineering Department, kept the contact alive until the corporate changes brought a more receptive atmosphere.

Further up the east side of San Francisco Bay, just north of Alameda, John Lorimer in 1920 began building

Diesels for the Atlas Imperial Company in Oakland. The Atlas Diesels soon found applications in drag line and scoop shovels, fishing boats, and locomotives. Atlas sent Henry J. Kaiser in the mid-1920s to see C. L. Best, Raymond C. Force, Starr, and Rosen. "If you won't put Atlas Diesels in your Caterpillar chassis," he reportedly said in frustration to Force one day, "then I will!"

Lorimer and his son Ralph Lorimer installed Atlas Diesels in Caterpillar and Monarch crawlers. Kaiser took three of the hybrids to a construction site on the Mississippi River. He discovered that the stationary-type Atlas en-

gines were meant for use in an application more structurally rigid and in an atmosphere more environmentally controlled than on an earth-moving crawler tractor. The heavy engines destroyed the Monarch and seriously stressed the Caterpillar 60 chassis to the breaking point.

But while Kaiser's experiences 2,000 miles away argued for a go-slow attitude, an event 12,000 miles away injected fresh fuel into the fire.

In early 1927, Henry Howard was working in the Export Department for Charles Parker Holt. Holt had arranged for a gas Model 60 and spare parts to be shipped

1931 Caterpillar Model 60 Diesel

Original owner Mark Weatherford kept good records. He turned over 149.8 acres per twenty-three-hour day—a total of 6,880 acres, at a cost of $535.81 for the entire job. The cost per acre was 7.8¢.

to Khartoum in the Anglo-Egyptian Sudan. The Gezira Plains, between the White Nile and Blue Nile rivers, was the second-largest cotton-producing area in the world.

"Heavy plowing in the early days, in many places, in sugar cane, in beets, even cotton was done with what's called cable tackle," Howard explained. "You have two tractors—steam engines—one on either side of the field. One has a big, winding drum under it and a cable. The

other one has a return pulley. You have a double cable that goes across the field and a two-way plow. You pull it across, you pull it back, and they advance down the field. So you plow out the whole thing with no headland.

"Best had hardly any exports, just to the Hawaiian Islands in cane sugar. But Holt ran these cable people off practically everywhere. These machines were made by British manufacturers, companies like J. and H. McLaren, from Leeds, or G. J. Fowler, from St. Ives. They were just about done; Holt had run them off.

"All of a sudden, there popped up a proposed competitive demonstration…in the cotton. A 60 against a cable system. It was figured that the 60 could run lengthwise in the fields. And while it would leave head lines in the turns, it would be more efficient than the steam-and-cable plowing, because Holt had run them off everyplace else….

"So this demonstration was set up. And Ted Farley went up there from South Africa. Ted Farley was the old Holt representative in Africa and he hadn't been home since the merger. He went up there to take over.

"Low and behold!. We got licked! Fowler showed up not with a steam tractor but with a tractor that had a Benz Diesel in it. Well, Farley cabled us and told us about it. And he requested that he [be allowed to] go up to Germany and buy one of these Benz engines.

"Farley was told to do that. I was clerking at the Export Department, saw it all. Farley placed the order and then he came home. I remember there were delays. Once Benz sent us a letter telling us they had been 'abandoned by their camshaft maker.' But the engine finally came and Caterpillar had it.

"And then Rosen—and certainly Starr, I don't know who else—designed the engine that came to be known as the D-9900, the Caterpillar Diesel engine."

Between clerking the order and the D-9900 prototypes, Howard was promoted and sent to Australia as Caterpillar's district representative. When he returned in 1931, Starr and Rosen had the prototype engine built and running.

Years afterward, C. L. Best told Hal Higgins about the early days with the Diesel: "We started experimenting with Diesel engines in the marketplace in 1932. In 1926, we decided to give all our engineering research to the Diesel. We spent over $1 million on the Diesel before ever marketing one."

"It's interesting about costs," Howard remarked. "Milt Davies worked in the lab in San Leandro at the time—later he became the director of research in Peoria. He told me that they initially built three engines. When they got the three engines built and running, the whole Board of Directors came out to the lab to find out how we could have spent $45,000 to build three engines!

"Now, I'm not going to tell you that Rosen's engine was a Chinese copy of the Benz engine because I don't believe it was," Howard said, smiling. "[But] they were both four-cylinder engines. They were both four-cycle engines. And they both were pre-combustion-chamber engines. And they both used Bosch fuel-injection equipment….

"The fuel injection thing was interesting. We were buying Bosch equipment and having trouble with the injection barrels being bell-mouthed, not seating properly. We kept

digging at Bosch about it and we finally got a letter out of them—now this is gossip I can't prove it because I never saw the letter—saying that Bosch couldn't correct this condition. Well, this was what we wanted all along. So we started building them ourselves in the basement of the administration building in San Leandro. We set up a bunch of German toolmakers—watchmakers, that's what I was told. They got the program going, just going fine. Then the war came later. We lost all the German watchmakers. But we had this procedure all worked out. So we got housewives in and they did just as well as the watchmakers. It just worked fine...."

Gordon Webster worked for the experimental section of the Engineering Department in the late 1920s and early 1930s when the first Diesels were installed in a Model 60 chassis. Years later, he recalled some experiences for Terry Galloway. From the beginning, methods of starting the Diesel

engine had to be made as foolproof as the engine itself. Gasoline "pony" engines were used almost from the start.

"They started up the gas engine with a flat belt," Webster explained, "ran it hot and piped the hot water through the Diesel to warm it up. When the Diesel was hot, the valves were dropped and the Diesel was run for a period to heat it up enough to stabilize the combustion process. It was important to quickly disconnect the belt between the gas engine and the Diesel. Because when that Diesel 'took off,' it would tear the gas engine to pieces."

After Kaiser's experience with the Atlas Diesel flexing and over-stressing the Caterpillar 60 chassis, the Engineering Department knew it had to strengthen the frame as well as solve all the other engineering problems.

"The 60 frame was dropped on the ground," Webster recalled, "and it was driven out back to test the power by dragging heavy frames around. This field test was a few blocks south of the plant. A special 'big' transmission was finally used for the Diesel engine tractors. It was geared down more for the Diesel than was normal for the old spark-ignition gas engines."

Once the problems were sorted out, the advantages—which Kaiser understood earlier and better than most—became clear. In 1932, gas for agriculture sold for 14–16¢ per gallon, whereas Diesel fuel was available at 4–7¢ a gallon. In early field tests, the Diesel 60 prototypes performed well under a heavy workload while consuming only four gallons per hour.

Mark Weatherford was an early purchaser of one of the Diesels for his Fairview Ranch in Arlington, Oregon; he took delivery of no. 1C12 early in March 1932. Out of his own curiosity, he kept detailed records of his first work with the tractor. Between March 4 and April 27, 1932, Weatherford plowed 6,880 acres using an Oliver twelve-bottom 16in plow and averaging 149.8 acres per 23hr day. He used a total of 5440gallons of Diesel fuel that cost 7 1/2¢ per gallon. Adding in all the other costs of lubricating and transmissions oils and one $2.99 repair, it cost him $535.81 for the entire job, or $0.0778 per acre. Weatherford estimated that 1C12 saved him $600 in fuel costs alone over his previous year with a 60hp gas tractor.

As the success of Caterpillar's Diesels became known, Rosen became a celebrity, delivering more than a dozen separate research papers between 1932 and 1935. Most significant to technical listeners and farmers were the performance characteristics of the Diesel. Rosen emphasized the engine's lugging ability, and stressed that its "rated load" was usually well below its peak load capacity, which gave operators a wide margin of power for a tough situation. Its torque curve really exemplified the difference between gasoline engines and the Diesel: Reducing engine speed by 5 percent increased torque 10 percent in the Diesel but improved gas engine torque by only 2.5 percent. This indicated the Diesel's superior ability to pull itself out of difficulty without greatly reducing engine speed to increase torque.

The Diesel seemed the answer to every operator's needs. Howard remembered the first dozen being assembled at San Leandro under Starr's critical scrutiny: "Each of the first twelve tractors was sent out with a beautiful mahogany box with a screwed-on top, containing a full set of replacement fuel pumps, valves, and lines, it being thought that these items might be needed early on. Oscar Starr was very specific about how, where, and to whom those tractors would be sold. They were to be sold for work approved by him, and to buyers close at hand [so] that the company could readily get to them in case of need.

"And so the great day came. We were all prepared to have the public batter down the doors and knock us down to get the Diesel 60. So we opened the door just slightly—and there was no one there.

"One or two went to Hawaii, to Theo H. Davies for the cane plantations; Arthur Rosen went with him. There they did all right, but Arthur Rosen soon learned that the heavier Diesel model with horsepower no greater than the gas model was less effective on the hillsides. In order to satisfy the users, he had to let out a little string, and so Arthur Rosen committed the original sin: He opened up the smoke screw [allowing more fuel into the mix], as did many another engineer and mechanic after him.

"Nine of those first two dozen went to Eygen-Bilsen, Belgium, in the spring of 1932, and Milt Davies—who went on to become director of research—went over there to attend to them. The job was excavating the Albert Canal.

"Selling the Diesel 60 was a tough job. And it sold hard, believe me. Nobody wanted to be first or early. I remember making a summary of the sales of all the different models. They all increased a little as we came out of the Depression. But the 60 lagged all the way."

Sales grew slowly. Caterpillar sold more of them in 1936 than in the previous four years combined. Production was up to 1,000 Diesel engines a month, so for 1937, the goal was set for 1,500 per month.

"The company made a mistake," Fred Lewis told Higgins. Lewis spent thirty years of his life in service and sales first for C. L. Best and then for Caterpillar in the United States and overseas. Much of his career was spent attending to the Diesels. "We sold these early Diesels with the idea that they would run on any fuel. I remember going up to one on a road job in Nevada and when I opened it up finding a ball of sulphur and wax as big as my fist in it. They had scooped up some old road oil from a patch that had been left from a paving job. I spent five years of the toughest troubleshooting I ever encountered in thirty years in that work. Every Diesel sent out had to be followed up and serviced."

And then real problems started to appear. Engine problems. Everywhere. Piston rings stuck. Cylinder walls scored. Main bearings burned up.

"We had about 3,000 Diesels in the field," Howard said. "Art Rosen got on it strong. They noticed that engines running in the West on West Coast oils—oils with paraffin bases, rather than the asphaltic-based oils from the East—didn't have as much ring sticking.

"[In a cooperative effort with] Standard Oil of California, G. B. Neely, the engineer, and Rosen developed the first detergent oil, compound oils, called 'Delo.'

"Well, they couldn't get any distribution on it," Howard shrugged, remembering the spirit of cooperation that collided with the spirit of competition. "So Caterpillar put all their dealers in the oil business selling this detergent [oil] all over the country. Then we developed a single-cylinder test engine to develop new lubricants. We just gave them away to everybody."

He shook his head in irony. "I'm telling you, in that time, to send a Diesel-powered oil-well-drilling engine rig out on a Texaco lease, and to tell them that they had to use California Standard oil or California Shell oil, when you knew—and couldn't tell them—that Texaco was working on a new detergent oil…. Oohhh, it was an exciting time to be working at Caterpillar."

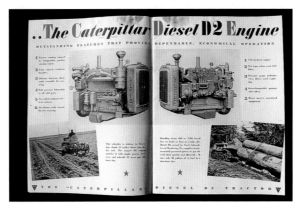

1934 Caterpillar Diesel Model 50
Above, when the Diesel 50 was tested at University of Nebraska in late May 1933, it achieved a record for fuel efficiency, 14.12hp-hours per gallon.

Left, inside the D2 brochure

Chapter 9

Decisions, Decisions

Hi-Way Yellow Becomes Caterpillar's Color ✦ *Changes in Model Nomenclature* ✦ *D For Diesel, R for Roosevelt*

In late 1931, came the inter-office memo heard around the world: "Beginning Monday, December 7, all Caterpillar tractors and all Caterpillar road machines shipped from the factories will have as their standard color Hi-Way Yellow. This is a rich, golden shade of yellow, bright, and lustrous. Trademarks and trimmings are black. A very thorough study of the subject of paint on the part of our own organization and the country's leading color and paint authorities resulted in the choice of Hi-Way Yellow as the standard color. It has been chosen with full consideration of every factor—attractiveness of appearance, the safety factor of high-visibility use, the legal requirements in certain localities for machines used on the highways, durability of paint, and protection of the surface."

The final paragraph of the letter gave away a little secret that only the few who were privy to the decisions really understood: "Road machines can be supplied in colors other than Hi-Way Yellow at the extra cost shown in the current price list. Unless your orders specify otherwise, you will be supplied with tractors and road machines of the above color hereafter. Purchases of tractors will now have the option, at no extra cost, of Silver Gray, trimmed in black—a lighter, brighter, and more attractive shade of gray than has been standard in the past. However, if this color is desired, your orders must so specify otherwise, tractors will be painted Hi-Way Yellow. The present gray, or any other colors other than Hi-Way Yellow and Silver Gray, may be had at the extra charge shown in the current price list."

Howard reread the memo sixty years later and recalled the events leading up to it: "The yellow paint? It's a very good example of how a well-managed corporation makes an executive decision," he said. And then he smiled broadly. "You determine the problem. You examine the alternatives. And you seek the best one."

"What happened was that Walter Gardner, the advertising manager, said, 'Look, we're trying to get out of the Depression here. Why don't we brighten these tractors up?

We're painting them this damned dull grey with red trim. Already, two states are specifying color! Missouri uses silver, Kansas uses a kind of orange.'

"The idea they were using," Howard said, "was to increase the visibility of the darned things. So people wouldn't hit them. Grey things were hard to see. So, it was considered kind of a good idea. Herb Mee was my boss, vice-president in charge of sales, and he formed a committee. Walter Gardner, Ed Galvin [sales manager], and some others. They examined the matter and they had three 30s painted up. One was a deep orange with a black engine, very handsome tractor. One was yellow and one was aluminum!

"The committee met. Discussed. Evaluated. And it settled on the multi-colored tractor—orange with black—and told the Manufacturing Department that this was what they wanted. And the Manufacturing Department just turned around and said, 'We won't do it.' And in those days, when the Manufacturing Department spoke, you listened. You didn't shove the Manufacturing Department around, believe me. So we said, 'All right, then, we'll have the aluminum.' Fine. They put that in the paint booths and they had some trouble handling it. And they came back and said, 'We won't do that, either.' So we said, 'All right, then, we'll have the yellow.' Fine. See, smooth corporate decision making.

"Of course, it went on and of course, it became known as Caterpillar Yellow. The Air Force adopted it. Eventually all construction machinery adopted it. International Harvester changed over from red to yellow. It used to be said that we couldn't make any money on the tractors so we sold paint."

But road construction safety yellow was not universally welcomed. Dealer and agent reactions varied. Willard Shepard, Caterpillar's dealer in Los Angeles, had once been Holt Manufacturing's factory manager. He and his sales staff were prodigious producers. Twice a year, Shepard sent in an order that the factory valued highly: twenty two-ton tractors, sold in the San Fernando Valley to the orange

1929 Caterpillar

1929 Caterpillar Model 10

Opposite page, Doug Veerkamp, left, his son, Matt, 11, and his grandfather, George Wagner, 94, swap stories around Doug's 1921 Best Model 30. In the background, the 1929 Caterpillar Model 60 with the disk sits near the little 1929 Model 10.

1929 Caterpillar Model 10
The Model 10, introduced in 1929, weighed 4,575lb. While it was still crank started, it offered the creature comfort of padded seats. The big Model 60 weighed 20,000lb and in low gear maximum draw tests, would nearly pull three Model 10s.

1939 Caterpillar Model 30

Caterpillar's Model 30 was renamed the Model R4. It used a Delco Remy generator and starter motor. This crawler is in the Joseph Heidrick, Sr, collection.

grove operators. That kind of volume earned Shepard considerable respect. And when the December 7 memo landed on Shepard's desk, he was furious. He responded with a telegram that became famous: "I'm not yellow. My men aren't yellow. And we won't sell yellow machines. Hereafter—and until further notice—paint the old colors at extra charge."

Within a year, however, Shepard laughed about it and Los Angeles County saw its first Hi-Way Yellow Caterpillars.

Four years after the color change, Caterpillar changed its model nomenclature. Beginning in 1935, no longer was tonnage or horsepower used as the model name, and no longer did that same number mark the radiator's sides. For the Diesel-engined popular new series, Rudolf Diesel's initials were paired with a number to designate the tractor's size and power relative to that of other Caterpillar models. The RD8, RD7, and RD6 were followed by the RD4 in

1929 Caterpillar Model 15

Left, this model could have been called the 3-Ton as it weighed just 5,900lb. But Model 15s fit in between the 7,900lb Model 20 introduced a year earlier and the 4,575lb Model 10. The 15 was fitted with the four-cylinder 3.75x5.00in engine.

1939 Caterpillar Model 30

Lower right, the Model 30 and the R4 used Caterpillar's inline four-cylinder 4.25x5.50in engine, producing a maximum 37.8 brake horsepower at 1400rpm. It sold for $1,925. The diesel-engine version, D4—with a fuel-injection system and gas starting engine—was introduced for $2,475 in the late 1930s.

1929 Caterpillar Model 10

Lower left, the Model 10 used Holt's 3.625x4.00in L-head four-cylinder engine. At 1500rpm, it produced 10 drawbar and 14 belt pulley horsepower. In first gear at 2mph. the 4,000lb Model 10 pulled 2,816lb.

1936. Standard gasoline-engined tractors were simply labeled the R series. Some designations were abbreviated further, to the letter D alone (for "Diesel") in 1937, and the D2 followed the long line begun with the Holt two-ton prior to the consolidation.

This is the popular story of the meaning of those letters R, D, and RD, and it is supported by factory memoranda. Unfortunately, the little bit of historical documentation that still exists came well after the fact. So, maybe it didn't happen exactly that way.

Howard was there. And what he recalls is different. It is also much more provocative and fascinating in its characterization of the personalities involved: "Believe me, in the 1930s, sales were hard to get. And along in here, the Forest Service had some money. There was a tractor called the Cletrac Forty. It had been in existence for quite a little while. It was quite a lively little tractor. The Forest Service liked it very much, and they put a blade on the front of it, an angling blade very much like a grader blade that would roll the earth. We couldn't touch it. We had nothing.

"Now, I don't know who had the idea. I'm not going to take the credit for it. I think it was [B. Claude] Heacock. His suggestion was, 'We oughta take a small tractor and hang a big engine on it. Put the gas 50 engine on a small

chassis.' He took it up to Manufacturing and Engineering. Neither wanted to do it. But he was the president. He told them to do it. We conferred with the Forest Service and they were interested. Their only change was that they wanted a foot-operated clutch, not a hand one. So we got this tractor ready and it came out at about 250lb to the drawbar horsepower. It was a hell of a lively machine.

"We put a LaPlant-Choate 'Trail Blazer' blade on it, and Warren Peterson, the demonstrator for LaPlante-Choate, said it was the best bulldozer tractor he'd ever seen. It was lively; it wasn't stodgy like the other Caterpillars were. And then came the name of it.

"Oscar Starr was the boss. And boy was he ever. I saw that I had a chance, so I said to this room full of managers and executives, 'Gentlemen, you've got to put a new name on this tractor, but there are some things I think you should reconsider. Holt called their tractors by weight; Best called them by nominal horsepower, not drawbar horsepower. Now, when the tractor gets a little stronger, you tell the customer it's got more than 60hp they complain because you still call it a 60. Holt's embarrassment with the weight was that they had a five-ton model and Monarch had a six-ton. Holt would go to the county, for example, and say that our tractor weighed pretty near six tons. 'Why do you call it a five ton, then?' Now, I suggest to you that you give the tractor a name that means absolutely nothing—so that you can invest your advertising money in it year after year after year.'

"They thought that this was a good idea. Now, I should tell you, Claude Heacock had a visceral hatred for Roosevelt—the New Dealer not the Rough Rider. He made public statements—awful—to the point that in the state of Indiana, they considered boycotting Caterpillar products. He would never shut up about it. Everybody knew how he felt. And here Heacock wanted to call this new tractor the 'Roosevelt 50'!

"Well, nobody said a word. We were all just speechless. So, finally, I had to speak up. And I said, 'Claude, look, you're gonna kill us! The Roosevelt thing will be a source of continual embarrassment.' I just couldn't figure it! 'And you don't want 50 either. Because we don't know what it is....'

"Well, there was some more discussion, and he finally settled for the 'R5.' And that's what it became! We started bidding it, and we sold a whole pot full of them, a lot of them to the Forest Service. I think we even may have sold some commercially. It was a hell of a tractor because it was lively."

The issue of nomenclature came up again and again. When new engines were introduced and installed in tractors, the Marketing, Sales, and Advertising Departments wanted some new designation, some manner by which to differentiate it from the existing machines.

"We had the old, the first, Rosen Diesel engine," Howard explained. "But we also had a new line of engines for the Engine Division. [They had a bore and stroke of] 5.25x8.00in, [and were available in] six, four, and three cylinders: D-11000, D-7700, [and] D-5500. That went into the big tractor, and it was called the 70. And Oscar Starr, who loved to design engines, also designed a new gas engine for it; it was known as the 9900-G.

"Very few of those were sold. On a bid, I sold one to the Panama Canal Authority. But that was the 70. Then after a while, they built it up to the 75. And they were going to goose up the D-13000 with the 5.75in bore—that was the 75. They were going to goose it up [and] rename the tractor. I think they were going to call it the 80.

"Again, I argued. It made no sense. Using those numbers trapped us. It made us look less than honest when the next improvement came out. It went round and round. So they came up with the '8' and then 'RD.' And that was Heacock's work. 'D' was Diesel and he kept that Roosevelt 'R,' and why, I can't tell you.

"This tractor had the name 'Eighty' cast on the radiator. I remember they took a hand grinder and ground it off and painted 'RD8' for the show the next day. And that's where it came from. I was there. I sat there in the middle of it. And I still can't explain why."

1929 Caterpillar Model 15

Left, at 1250rpm, the L-head engine produced 21.3 drawbar and 24.8 belt pulley horsepower. In drawbar tests, it pulled 2,179lb at nearly 3mph top speed in second gear. This example was restored and is owned by Fred Heidrick, Sr.

1935 Caterpillar Model 22

Below, the Model 22 was introduced in 1934 as the distillate fuel version of the Model R2 gas engine crawler. The 4.00x5.00in four-cylinder engine produced 19.3 drawbar and 27.2 belt horsepower at 1250rpm in University of Nebraska tests.

Chapter 10

Push Comes to Shove in World War II and Everywhere

The Fighting Seabees and Their Caterpillar Crawlers ✦ "Bullets Pinging into the Metal Blade" ✦ Birth of the "Bulldozer" ✦ LaPlante-Choate Builds the Blades

1935 Caterpillar Model RD6

Above, the RD6 is 11ft-3in long, 6ft tall without exhaust pipe, and 6ft wide. It weighs 13,900lb and in first gear pulls 8,749lb.

1935 Caterpillar Model RD6

Opposite page, as successors to the Diesel 35, 50, and 75, the RD6, RD7, and RD8 shared common cylinder bore and stroke. But the RD6 used a three-, the RD7 a four-, and the RD8 a six-cylinder engine.

Late in April 1942, the Japanese High Command launched a new offensive policy of expansion. The fact that this would occur eight time zones away—one-third of the way around the world—from Peoria still did not render it insignificant to Caterpillar. The first steps that the Japanese took were not the well-kept secrets that they might have hoped but their attack succeeded nonetheless. On May 3, Japan invaded the cities of Port Moresby in New Guinea and Tulagi in the Southern Solomon Islands. The Japanese intended to use New Guinea and the Solomons as bomber and seaplane bases from which to launch their eventual attack against Australia.

For Caterpillar, this was a threat of some concern. While Stockton was 6,000 miles to the northeast of the Solomons, the company's nearest branch in Australia was barely 600 miles away.

Defeating the Japanese at Midway upset their progress and the US High Command set out to keep them off balance for as long as possible. This worked to some extent. In the Solomons on August 7, American forces combined with New Zealanders and sailed into Tulagi Harbor to begin to recapture the island and especially Lunga Field, where the Japanese Air Corps had constructed a complete air base.

In the early morning of August 8, the ships rounded Guadalcanal from the west and steamed straight north into the harbor. They met strong, unexpected resistance. Aurelio Tassone, a US Navy Construction Battalion equipment operator, told Hal Higgins about the landing years later: "It was during the first hot hours of the invasion. There were ten of us Seabees attached to a New Zealand outfit aboard an LST. But our landing didn't go by the books at all. Instead of running in after the LCI's—the infantry landing craft—and finding the troops already holding the beach, our tank-landing ship carrying our bulldozers plowed in alone under heavy fire.

"Before we struck the shore, the Japanese scored a direct hit topside, wiping out an entire gun crew. Below on the tank deck, we bulldozer drivers felt the concussion and heard shrapnel slapping against the ship. Finally, the bow doors swung open, and right away we had our first view of combat. We could see dead Americans and New Zealanders washing back and forth in the surf. It was like a bad dream.

"We rolled those big dozers out on the sand as fast as we could and started working hard. We knew that the sooner we got our jobs done, the sooner the fighting men who were streaming ashore could push inland."

Tassone had swung his Caterpillar toward a gun emplacement, moving faster than he knew the tractor could move, digging with the bulldozer blade, he said, faster than he thought possible. Before he'd finished gouging the beach away from that first gun, his lieutenant, Charles Turnbull, got his attention. All around Tassone, the sounds of battle nearly drowned out the rumble of his tractor. Turnbull pointed at a pillbox terrorizing the LST that was unloading.

"'Hit that damned thing,' Turnbull yelled. 'Spread it all over the beach!'"

The pillbox was barely 100ft away, surrounded by logs jutting 2ft above the sand but which were deeply buried. The soldiers inside were firing twin-mounted 37mm guns that they supplemented with small arms fire.

"As I started the dozer across that hundred-foot stretch," Tassone explained, "I raised its blade to help protect myself from the fire that was pretty sure to turn my way. Sure enough, in a few seconds, I could hear the bullets that were meant for me pinging into the metal blade. I gave the machine all the speed she had. I remember seeing the sand bubbling up both sides like boiling water.

"Well, I got to the nest all right, and just as the dozer was going to hit it, I pressed the blade down as hard as it would go—I almost stalled the motor. The blade bit through the logs like they were snowdrifts. The gun mount toppled over, and chunks of logs and bodies flew up in the air. Everything was crushed and buried underneath that rip-roaring machine. Then I locked one track, meaning to

bear down again, but the lieutenant yelled for me to get away before I exploded any ammunition that might have been there.

"That's all there was to it. To tell the truth, I was surprised at the fuss naturally, I was tickled to get the Silver Star. But what I really got the biggest kick out of—later on—was learning that my little experiment had started somebody designing a tank that had an oversized dozer blade mounted on it for use against the pillboxes. I heard when the boys went ashore in Normandy, those new tank dozers saved a lot of good guys from dying. Could anybody want a sweller reward?"

A dictionary in the 1990s describes a bulldozer as any tractor with a front-mounted shovel or blade, used for pushing or moving earth or debris. Half a century earlier, its definition was more precise but also more suggestive. A bulldozer was: "An upsetting machine, as a forging or

1935 Caterpillar Model RD6
The RD6 retained the Diesel 40 three-cylinder 5.25x8.00in engine, first introduced on the Model 35. At 850rpm, it produced 38.7 drawbar and 48.1 belt horsepower.

bending press. The ram slides in a horizontal path and is actuated by a pair of powerful cranks and connecting rods."

While history—and Benjamin Holt—have been able to put a name to the originator of the term "Caterpillar" to refer to his crawler tractors, no one knows who watched the first blade-equipped crawler running into piles of earth and recognized the similarity to the action of the forge shop ram that pounded hot bars into shape.

It is possible that the shop piece took its name from the

earth mover. Hal Higgins became fascinated with the idea and researched its earliest versions that he heard about in Utah: "The Mormon Board was a flat, wooden scraper blade about 4 to 4-1/2ft wide by 2-1/2ft deep. It was attached to [the back end of a horse hitch] tongue by two iron or steel upward-curving drag connections." A. H. Ayers of the Utah Construction Company related to Higgins in a story that was then published in *Western Farm Life* in January 1950. "These Mormon Boards," Ayers went on, "were used with two horses to finish and trim the grade of the railroad or canal. They were first used, dragged behind the horse teams, in building the railroad across Wyoming and Utah in the 1880s. Since most of the contractors on that work were Mormons or employed Mormon laborers, the tongue scrapers developed by these people became known as 'Mormon scrapers.'"

Higgins learned that the shortcomings of the Mormon scraper led to its next iteration. The scraper worked adequately so long as the team could be kept in front and the material pulled into place. But it failed when material had to be pushed, for example, down a bank. That need led to the idea of mounting the board on a pole in the front of two oxen. Hence the name.

Oxen-dozer?

This bulldozer gained efficiency when the push board and pole were attached to wheels. Using the tongue and front running gear from a wagon to support the rear of the dozer, runners were fitted on the back of the board. This kept it from digging too deeply when pushing and supported it when the blade was backed away from the load. Still, controlling the oxen and the board was difficult. Tractor power vastly increased the use of bulldozer blades.

The April 19, 1862, issue of *Scientific American* published a linecut engraving of Brooks's Road Scraper, a road leveler drawn behind two oxen with a man walking behind the blade. According to the accompanying text, "While this scraper is believed to be as convenient and serviceable as any for digging cellars and canals and for other similar work, it is especially designed for road making. It will be seen that it moves the earth to the middle of the road with far greater ease and with less interruption of the work than the scrapers usually employed." Patented January 21, 1862, through the *Scientific American* Patent Agency, the magazine advised that persons seeking further information should contact the inventor, James F. Brooks, directly through general delivery at Stafford Springs, Connecticut.

Sometime in 1880, the Western Wheeled Scraper Company published a brochure promoting its "Western Bulldozer," which the company claimed replaced forty men. Its 2x4ft blade could be tilted. At the end of the 7ft, 7in tongue, the operator was seated above an axle with two 30in wheels that could be steered. The entire apparatus weighed 800lb.

Following the flooding in Stockton in the winter of 1908, workers at the Holt factory bolted a plank onto the front frame of one of their wheeled steam traction engines to remove debris from the streets. But neither Benjamin Holt nor C. L. Best took much interest in developing, manufacturing, or selling implements for their tractors. It fell to others to produce accessories.

Otto Zentner, an International Harvester dealer from Los Banos, California, spoke with Higgins in the mid-1940s. Zentner had firsthand experience in Milwaukee in the winter of 1924 with snowplows on Best 60s: He had used the first dozer blade that Ralph Choate designed specifically for a Best 30: "We set the dozer up on the Best in the Hunter Machinery Shop. Hunter was the Best dealer in Milwaukee. I got in the cab and started turning the tiller to raise the blade. No result. I got out and looked around to find the rear of the tractor 10in off the floor. The blade was too long and too heavy for the tractor. So we moved the entire assembly back, put a trunion axle across the swing frames, hinging it at that point. And then we added rub plates on the ends of the sprocket shaft. I added a ballast box on the rear for counter balance and we filled it with rocks. And I mounted a winch control on the drawbar and operated it through the cab window. We ran this contrap-

Starting the Caterpillar D6 with Rope Pull Engine Starter Motor

1. Be certain that the gear shift lever is in neutral. Be certain that the flywheel clutch is disengaged.
2. Set the throttle control lever forward and be certain it is locked in the "shut off" position. This lever also controls the opening and closing of the fuel injection pumps.
3. Set the compression release lever in the "start" position.
4. Disengage the starting engine clutch by pulling the control lever back toward the starting engine.
5. Open the starting engine fuel tank valve and pull out the choke control.
6. Pull out the throttle control, allowing the throttle to close.
7. Turn the ignition switch on.
8. Place the knotted end of the starting rope in one of the two notches on the starting engine flywheel flange, with the knot to the outside. Wind the rope around the groove in such a manner that pulling the rope will turn the flywheel in the direction indicated by the arrow on the flywheel.
9. Grasp the starting rope handle with one hand and spin the flywheel with a quick pull on the rope.
10. When the starting engine starts, allow it to idle long enough to distribute crankcase lubricating oil thoroughly before running at its governed speed.
11. The starting engine cranks the Diesel engine through a sliding pinion, which engages with the flywheel by pulling up on the starter pinion control. If the pinion does not engage readily, partially engage the starting engine clutch for an instant so that the teeth will mesh with the flywheel gear. The clutch is provided with a brake to stop the clutch shaft from turning. To apply the brake, pull the clutch lever all the way back.
12. After the pinion is engaged, push in the throttle control to let the starting engine run at full governed speed. Then engage the starting engine clutch by pushing the lever forward until it snaps over the center.

Note: The heat generated when the starting engine is cranking the Diesel engine against compression, and circulation of the starting exhaust around the Diesel engine inlet manifold warms the cylinders, pistons, and combustion chamber to the starting temperature. Move the compression release to the "run" position as soon as the starting engine is cranking the Diesel at normal cranking speed.

13. After the starting engine has cranked the Diesel engine against the compression for a few minutes and the temperature indicator shows the proper reading, pull out the plunger stop and pull the throttle control lever back about half way. If the engine does not fire after it has turned several revolutions, move the throttle to the extreme forward position with the plunger locked and let the starting engine turn the Diesel engine a little longer to raise its temperature.
14. When the Diesel engine begins to fire, the starter pinion automatically disengages. But it is necessary to disengage the starting engine clutch by pulling back on the control lever.
15. Stop the starting engine by closing the valve in the starting engine fuel tank line. Allow the engine to burn all the fuel in the carburetor. Then turn off the ignition switch.
16. Check the lubricating oil pressure gauge to see that it is registering. When the engine is warm, the gauge should register in the "operating range."

Note: Allow the Diesel engine to idle 5 minutes with the throttle at least half open and 5 minutes at full speed before applying the load.

tion for two weeks until the city decided to buy it."

Choate recalled manufacturing his first complete bulldozer in 1921 for an contractor who was building a road between Cedar Rapids and Dubuque, Iowa. The contractor was faced with removing rocks as large as office desks, and he asked Choate to see what he could do.

"We came back to Cedar Rapids [home of LaPlante-Choate's shops], and the bulldozer was born—just a plate of steel out in front of the tractor. I took it down to the job," Choate explained to Higgins, "with pride of achievement. And after the first attempt to bulldoze the rock, our bulldozer was a plain zero.

"'Now! Go back and build a good one,' the contractor demanded. But when he saw the second effort, the man summed up his opinion with a snort: 'I never saw such a conglomeration of bridge iron in my life!'

"We started beefing up our bulldozer," Choate confided, "by adding steel, by welding it to the sides of the bulldozer. We added enough steel to break the tractor instead of the dozer this time." Two years later, however, the experience paid off and Choate was producing tractor-mounted bulldozers, bucket loaders, and other load-moving and lifting devices as fast as he could turn them out.

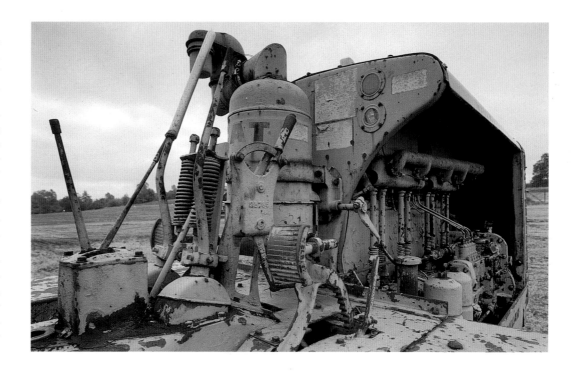

1937 Caterpillar Model RD7

Above, this crawler used the four-cylinder version of the 5.25x8.00in diesel engine, rated at 61hp at 850rpm. In May 1936 Nebraska tests, the RD7, weighing 21,020lb, was able to pull 16,782lb in low gear at 1.5mph. Peak brake horsepower measured 86.3 when engine speed was increased to 1000rpm.

1935 Caterpillar Model RD6

Left, RD6 production began in late 1935. Previously called the Diesel 40, the name changed for the 1936 model year. This crawler was restored and is owned by Dave Smith of Woodburn, Oregon.

Chapter 11

The Mountain Mover

Robert Gilmour LeTourneau ✦ *The Fine Art of Earth Moving* ✦
T. G. Schmeiser's Scraper ✦ *Electrics and Hydraulics Put to Work* ✦
Tournapulls ✦ *"Judgment Learned From Experience"*

It fell to another strong individual outside of the Best and Holt families to perfect the bulldozer that Ralph Choate had begun. But by the time Robert Gilmour LeTourneau was finished, he had elevated all of earth moving to an art form.

In 1900, when LeTourneau was twelve years old, he built his first earth mover. He elaborated on this in his autobiography, *R.G.LeTourneau: Mover of Men and Mountains*. "It was a heifer-pulled snowplow designed to get me out of several hours of opening paths with a shovel. It was a V-shaped affair with curving sides to thrust the snow up and to both sides, and it might have worked. The heifer kicked it and me to flinders before I could find out, curing me forever of any regard for animal power of any kind."

While the fate of his plow spared the world from heifer-dozers, it did nothing to diminish his interest in moving earth in other ways. He learned metallurgy in a foundry after quitting school in the eighth grade. At the turn of the century, metallurgy—in fact all of industry—had entered the next, highly accelerated stage of the Industrial Revolution. As the youngest apprentice working beneath two older boys, LeTourneau was learning something new every day. But overnight the classes changed. Where one day he watched his masters pouring pig iron, the next day they were mixing manganese and copper and countless other metals by the ounce to pour the alloys the customers demanded. As one of the apprentices described it, the old technology passed by "faster than time on your day off."

By 1905, every lesson he learned in welding and metal handling came with a lesson in human values and faith. A devoutly religious man, LeTourneau's philosophy was liberally seasoned with Christian ethics and insights. This was equally balanced with hard knocks, hard luck, and hard steel machines formed in his own mind and welded by his own hand.

LeTourneau had completely sworn off school by 1909, following four correspondence courses. But even with his limited education, he was overqualified for many of the jobs that interested him in construction, road building, and earth moving. He took a job tending stationary engines for the crews building a dam over the Stanislaus River in central California.

"Construction work in 1909 was man-killing in the full meaning of the term," LeTourneau wrote. "Steel beams still had to be man-handled when mule-drawn loads bogged down in the mud. Accidents on the ground were frequent even before the clumsy steam cranes began lifting the beams to the riggers waiting on the structure. The best of crane operators, jerking at a confusing array of long handles and tromping on foot pedals, was lucky to line up a beam within inches of where it was to be placed, after which the riggers, working with no safety devices or nets, had to use their own weight to get it into position. The steel hanger with three years' experience was greatly admired in those days—not for his skill, [but] for his survival."

In those days, everything was difficult, challenging, and crude. Tolerances may have been tight but the equipment was coarse. LeTourneau put in his share of time operating a Fresno, basically a mule-powered scoop shovel patented by James Porteous in 1882. A four-mule team pulled a 5ft-wide Fresno scraper along the ground on its bottom until it arrived at the point where the operator began to scoop earth. The handle of the Fresno was an iron bar as long as 8ft. Lifting up the handle tilted the blade forward. The mules protested, but the best mule-skinners—those operators as effective with a bullwhip as with the Fresno in dirt—could scoop up just about half a cubic yard of dirt by bearing down onto the handle to lift the blade out of the ground. If everything worked smoothly, four strong mules and a good skinner could move 100 cubic yards of dirt the length of a football field in a 9hr workday.

In 1912, LeTourneau was twenty-four. Working as an automobile garage mechanic, he watched the appearance of one innovation after another. Self-starter motors quickly caught his eye, and entranced by electricity, he began thinking about them while a friend of his tried to make one

Best 60 with Schmeiser Scraper
A Best 60 works with a Schmeiser scraper. The scraper had long racks on either side driven by reduction gears and electric motors. These were powered by the electric motor mounted on the pedestal on Caterpillar, driven off the flywheel. Higgins collection

1945 Caterpillar Model D8 with Caterpillar Model 80 Scraper
Opposite page, in 1945, the D8 sold new for $6,950 and gave owners and operators traction in the rough.

1928 Caterpillar Model 60 with

LeTourneau "Hi-Boy"

LeTourneau's "Hi-Boy" 7cu-yd Scraper

was the largest at the time. This was the

35th scraper sold. With solid steel

wheels, it went for about $4,250 with

Power Control unit.

for his own Ford automobile. That this energy, created by a generator run from storage batteries or by a gasoline engine could do such things as turn over an engine, that a small motor could rotate four or six pistons in cylinders, fascinated him. LeTourneau began to imagine that there might be other uses for these strong, small motors.

Five years later, in 1917, he married Evelyn Peterson, a seventeen-year-old who had mechanically minded brothers, including Howard Peterson, the eldest, and Buster, the youngest. One year after his wedding, repairing a 75hp Holt for a customer, he came across his first land-leveler scraper. At the same time he thought it was both ugly and

the most fascinating piece of equipment he'd ever seen. It was adjusted by belts and gears operated by a man riding on the scraper.

After repairing the scraper, the customer hired Le-Tourneau to level forty acres. The marriage between tractor operator and scraperman must be made in heaven. If not, one or the other can make the partner's life hellish. Le-Tourneau's first scraper job was not pleasant, but years later, he reassessed its effect on him: "By the second day, I knew I had found a job which satisfied me like no other in my life. I wanted to move dirt. Lots of dirt."

Soon after finishing the job—and losing money be-

1953 Caterpillar D4

Left, after ripping the soil, Ed Akin operates the D4 and LeTourneau scraper to deepen a reservoir. The Model D scraper will carry 3.5yd.

1953 Caterpillar D4

Below, five-speed transmission provided a top speed of 5.4mph. Dick Akin of Placerville, California, owns this restored crawler.

cause of the mistakes he made—he began seriously to seek out earth moving work. He borrowed $1,000 and bought a 1915 Holt 75 and rented a friend's Schmeiser scraper.

In 1915, T. G. Schmeiser of Fresno, California, had received a patent for his scraper with a blade that was raised and lowered by compressed air. It could move 3 cubic yards of dirt at nearly 3mph, but like the belt-operated scrapers, the compressed-air Schmeisers had problems in rock or among tree roots. Belts slipped, gear teeth were stripped, or compressed-air hoses burst. But despite its drawbacks, it gave LeTourneau a kind of freedom, and he put Howard Peterson, just thirteen at the time, to work helping him repair his equipment before and after each job.

"No longer was I just a hired hand," LeTourneau exulted. "I was a land-leveling contractor with my own mortgaged machinery. And The Islands [an area of the San Joaquin River delta] were loaded with ranchers ready to pay the going price of $7.50 an hour for the man with a tractor and scraper."

R. G. LeTourneau with Holt 75 and Gondola

Above, from these humble beginnings, sitting on his Holt 75 trailing his Gondola, Robert G. LeTourneau nearly singlehandedly revolutionized earth moving. Higgins collection

Caterpillar 60 with Scraper

Right, was it an early bulldozer or an early scraper? Or was it a tractor-mounted Mormon board? Higgins collection

Ranchers supplied the scraper operator and in a 14hr day, LeTourneau made $100—provided he found an operator willing to work those long days. None would. LeTourneau began thinking as he listened to the drone of the Holt engine. He watched its big flywheel spin just inches away from his feet. The Holt's rumble sparked his imagination. Starting its big engine reminded him of his friend's starter motor for his Ford, and he wondered whether a DC motor could be rewired as a generator. It could run by belt off the flywheel spinning at his feet. He could wire the generator to an automobile starter motor and connect it by a pinion gear to a rack mounted on the scraper. If he put a motor on each side, he could tilt the blade for custom work. A switch at the operator's seat would raise or lower the scraper. It would just take one man working by himself, with no scraper operator to complain about long days.

After two weeks of those kinds of long days scraping customers' ground with an impatient ranch hand, LeTourneau worked even longer nights with Peterson. Soon he had an electric Schmeiser scraper. The leveled land was

1939 Caterpillar D7 with

LeTourneau Model M Carryall

Don Hunter's D7 idles in front of his

LeTourneau Carryall scraper. Hunter's

D7 was the 13th one manufactured.

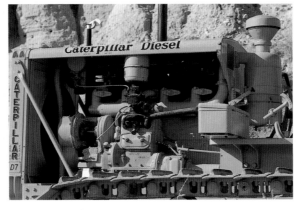

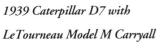

1939 Caterpillar D7 with

LeTourneau Model M Carryall

The D7 engine is a four-cylinder 5.75x8.00in I-head design with total displacement of 831ci. In its Nebraska tests in October 1940, it produced 75.8 drawbar horsepower at 1000rpm. In low gear, the 24,790lb crawler pulled 21,351lb at 1.33mph.

1939 Caterpillar

Model D2 with Murray Scraper

Next page, Ed Akin works on a small lake with his D2 and 2cu-yd Murray scraper. The four-cylinder 3.75x5.00in. Diesel produced 25.2 drawbar horsepower at 1525rpm.

smoother than the job done with a man riding the scraper, and LeTourneau's competitors came first to watch and then to try to persuade him to build one for them.

But LeTourneau knew how he worked. For him, each model was a prototype; the successive model, the one that was supposed to be the "working version," contained enough improvements to be yet another prototype. And so it went for decades. LeTourneau sold his first electric Schmeiser and built another. With it—a 3 cubic yard electric scraper—he completed a half-mile racetrack for the Stockton County Fair quicker even than he expected, earning him the right to display his machine next to the newest

offerings of C. L. Best and Benjamin Holt. He anticipated a lot of sales. Instead, he got advice.

"B. S. Harris of Harris Harvesters came up to me after my demonstration. 'A nice machine, son,' he said, 'when you get the flaws ironed out, if you don't kill yourself first.'"

Still young, LeTourneau bristled. As gently as possible, Harris pointed out the problems that he saw with Le-Tourneau's scraper. It had limited turning ability and for LeTourneau to serve as scraper operator as well as tractor driver required gymnastics.

1939 Caterpillar

Model D2 with Murray Scraper

*Above, with five forward speeds, the
7,420lb Model D2 could gear down
in first to pull 5,903lb. Top speed was
5.1mph, making efficient use of the
small, rubber-tired Murray scraper.*

1945 Caterpillar Model D8 with

Caterpillar Model 80 Scraper

*Right, the D8-1H series introduced in
1935, are 15ft-3in long, 7ft- 6in tall,
and 8ft-8in wide.*

"'When you make a machine for yourself,' Harris summed up, 'that's your baby and you won't mind if it cries. It's your brainchild and you're proud of it. But the contractor that buys it won't stand for its crying.'"

This polite professional critique reinforced LeTourneau's conviction that development work never is completed. And so for years to come, each successive machine was simply the next prototype. LeTourneau was motivated as much by an abiding desire to move more dirt as by his continuously curious nature. He found answers in boats that inspired him to cradle and surround his load. Adding a front plate to his scraper to enclose the dirt—to limit spillage—he named it the "gondola." If maximum loads had grown to one ton, were three possible? If three could be carried, then eight? If eight, then sixteen or twenty?

Twenty tons were now possible. The Mountain Mover was born from a telescoping water cup; LeTourneau's bucket telescoped to let the force of the loading dirt actually extend the wagon in sections to carry even more dirt.

If two motors let him remove the extra man, could more motors simply power the scraper and could he remove the extra piece of equipment in front of the scraper, the tractor? The

result would be one less machine to manage, to operate, to maintain. Could he make the scraper be the tractor as well?

"I had it all figured out," he explained in his autobiography. "I built four big, steel wheels, and into the hub of each wheel I installed a secondhand electric car motor, geared so that it would cause the wheel to turn around it. Those were pretty big wheels that would be hard to steer in mud, so I geared another electric car motor to the front wheels to give me electric steering. Two more motors went to power the five telescoping buckets. For their supply of electricity, I welded a big Navy-surplus generator to the front of the machine, and powered that with a Locomobile auto engine.

"No clutches, no transmission, no brakes. Just flexible electric cable to carry the power to each motor. Nothing for the operator to do but push buttons, occasionally pouring a little more gas to the Locomobile in hard going."

It worked. But it was slow: 1mph. Yet it lifted the load off the ground. It eliminated the friction; there was no longer a bucket or a scraper dragging the earth to impede movement once the bucket was filled. Slow as it was, it went along with him to Crow Canyon to build a highway between Oakland and Stockton. It was his first job as a large contractor, and it was on that job in 1926 that Le-Tourneau improved on another existing prototype, one that had been around since 1862.

When he dumped his scraped loads near the edge of

1941 Caterpillar Model D8 with

Caterpillar Model 80 Scraper

Above, Doug Veerkamp operates Ed Akin's 1954 D8-13A with a LeTourneau 4ft ripper, opening up soil to deepen a reservoir. The Model 13A weighed 37,150lb.

1941 Caterpillar RD8 with

LeTourneau blade

Right, Dick Railing's late-production RD8 is another well-used, well-worn Caterpillar with half a century of daily use. The 10ft wide LeTourneau bulldozer blade was operated by a rear-mounted Power Control unit, its cable fed forward through the well-known "headache" tube.

the canyon to be filled, he knew that the job still required men with shovels and wheelbarrows or mules with plow boards fastened to the fronts of their hitches. That system worked fine until it came time to back away from the edge and fill the blade with another load to push forward.

"Stuck up there in Crow Canyon," LeTourneau wrote, "my contribution was the first practical blade that could be raised or lowered at will, with push-button controls. I put a steel scraper blade out in front of my new Best tractor, rigged it up with an electric cable winch, and wove the cable through some sheaves. A press of a button would lift the blade out of the ground for easy turning or backing up. Touch the button again—shut off the power—and the blade would fall and dig into the ground of its own weight."

LeTourneau never rested on his laurels. Each development was the catalyst that sparked the next, and a large percentage of earth-moving science and technology sprang from his mind. It grew from his fingertips and took shape under his welding torches. He often was years ahead of everyone else in identifying a need and finding an answer.

1945 Caterpillar Model D8 with Caterpillar Model 80 Scraper
Left, D8s were powered by the D-13000 six-cylinder 5.75x8.00in engine.

1945 LeTourneau Tournapull Carryall LS
Below, when R. G. LeTourneau introduced his Tournapulls, skeptics asked him where was the rest of it. The inventor succeeded in turning the scraper into its own tractor.

"Without knowing it at the time," LeTourneau explained, "I was in a remarkable position in 1928 and one that gave me an advantage over my competitors. As a contractor, I was able to see all the weaknesses of the earth-moving machinery then in use, and as a manufacturer, I was able to do something about it." He understood the limits he reached with any piece of his own equipment, and he recognized and understood why the equipment imposed those limits. The next step was always meant to stretch the limits.

"The most serious problem facing me in building a big machine was lack of power," he continued. "The tractor manufacturers had some notion their machines were as powerful as they could get. Back when I was building Henry Kaiser's factory, we tried to interest a tractor com-

pany in building a machine with Diesel power.

"'I'll build my own,' Kaiser said, and he did, installing an Atlas Diesel in the frame of an old tractor. I finished the factory job on his first Diesel tractor, by equipping it with my electric generators. For a while there, we were really moving dirt. What we had overlooked was that the Diesel engine as then built was a stationary engine. Its separate cylinder blocks couldn't take the banging and wrenching they got in an uncushioned tractor. We blew out so many pistons we had to scrap the engine. And at that time, the tractor people, instead of noting the superior performance of the Diesel while it lasted, pointed to its failure and dropped the subject with relief."

LeTourneau incorporated in 1929 at nearly the same time as the Crash on Wall Street. But he was too busy building to take the time to look for something to jump off. Boulder Dam was to be built, and LeTourneau was one of the first contractors signed. His history was a syncopated overlapping cycle: Conceive, design, manufacture, move earth, develop, experiment, move more earth, remanufacture, construct, succeed, fail, rethink, assemble. This process led to the ultimate LeTourneau development, one that truly revolutionized earth moving.

It was the summer of 1932. Howard Peterson was supposed to demonstrate a steel-wheeled scraper to a potential

C. L. Best 30hp with LaPlante-Choate Bulldozer

A second-generation LaPlante-Choate bulldozer was mounted on this Best 30hp in Milwaukee. The large screw barely discernible at rear lifted or dropped the blade. Higgins collection

1945 LeTourneau

Tournapull Airborne Unit

Right, the Power Control unit, driven by shaft drive off the engine, operated three 3/8in cable drums, not the usual two drums of 1/2in cable. One drum controlled the dozer blade, another did the lift and depth control for the scraper, and the third controlled the ejector to dump the load.

1945 LeTourneau

Tournapull Airborne Unit

Below, LeTourneau used a Continental four-cylinder 162ci gasoline engine to drive the front wheels through a three-speed gearbox. Front tires were Caterpillar standard motor grader size whereas rears were light-truck 6.50x16s.

customer, Nick Basich, a contractor. Basich had a highway construction job in the southern California desert about fifty miles southeast of Palm Springs.

Peterson reconstructed the events that took place down near Indio alongside the Salton Sea: "It was hot. It was real hot. The dealer down there furnished the tractor and we brought the scraper. LeTourneau sent me down there to demonstrate. We hooked everything up and I started out, and the minute I put the scraper into the ground to try to get some dirt, the thing just bogged down in the sand until the wheels came off the ground and some kind of vibration was actually making them spin backwards.

"I called LeTourneau and said, 'This won't work here.

You just can't pull it with a tractor in this sand.' He told me to let him do a little thinking about it and he'd call back. He got hold of some tiremaker—Firestone, I think—and found out that the biggest tire they made was a 13.20x24.00in rim. [It was] a big truck tire, inflated to 90lb.

"So Bob [LeTourneau] said he'd make a set of wheels for the back end of that scraper and he was going to put dual rubber 13.20x24.00s on it, [with] hub[s] that [would] fit the axles. 'I can have this done in a couple of days,' he said.

"'You just stay there,' Bob said, 'and we'll send a truck right down with these tires and wheels all mounted and ready for you to slip on the axles.' So they arrived, we put them on, and they worked really well. But then the front ones sunk. They were smaller diameter and had a smaller face. So I called him and told him, and he said to stay there, he'd machine up another set of wheels and we'd put single 13.20x24.00s on the front. They arrived, we mounted them up, and it worked great.

"Well, the news got around that we put rubber tires on a scraper, and they all laughed at us," Peterson said. "They asked, 'What are you going to do when you hit rocks? They'll tear the tires all to pieces.'"

(Using rubber tires on tractors was not a new idea at this time. In 1846—eighty-five years earlier—R. W. Thomson had invented the air tire in Scotland. He fitted these tires to his own carriage which he used on Edinburgh's cobblestone roads. Within fifteen years, he had begun fitting 4in- to 5in-thick solid rubber bands onto steam traction engines to increase their traction and decrease the amount of damage they caused to the cobblestone roads. Williamson steamers, built under license at Grant Locomotive Works in Patterson, New Jersey, were fitted with Thomson rubber and then sold in California by an aggressive dealer in Stockton as early as 1871. Wider use of inflatable rubber tires began with Harvey Samuel Firestone's own efforts to put rubber on agricultural tractors. Allis-Chalmers became interested first, in 1931, even promoting tractor races at state and county fairs using Indianapolis 500 racer Barney Oldfield to show off the speed and smooth ride on Allis' rubber-shod Model U tractors.)

As LeTourneau continued to develop larger scrapers to run on rubber tires, he ran up against tougher resistance from manufacturers than from any rock wall he'd encoun-

tered. Peterson recalled some of the obstacles: "Fitting airplane tires didn't work; they simply did not offer enough puncture resistance," he explained. So LeTourneau approached the tire manufacturers. "The tire people refused to make any tires large and strong enough of conventional design on speculation. So, broke as we were, we gave the Firestone Company an order for $1 million worth of 18.00x24.00s. They said a million was what it would take to assure them a return for molds and manufacturing costs."

In late 1934, LeTourneau moved his operations east to Peoria to be closer to Caterpillar. His reliance on Caterpillar power had begun with his first Holt 75 with its scraper. Since then, Best, Holt or Caterpillar crawlers had pulled and pushed all of his inventions. This move offered him

1945 LeTourneau
Tournapull Airborne Unit
Steering the Tournapull was by individual wheel clutches (the matching tall levers next to the gear shift). Levers by the seat controlled the cable Power Unit affecting the dozer and scraper. Operating this model, especially downhill, was treacherous.

Ted Schmeiser leans against the rear

wheel hub of a 1910 Best 70hp tractor

with Buffalo Pitts six-cylinder engine.

Schmeiser linked a tractor-mounted

compressed-air pump to a tank back on

his first Land Leveller.

Higgins collection

Starting the LeTourneau Airborne Unit

1. Walk around entire machine. Visually inspect for broken or worn parts, or damaged or worn cables to the bulldozer blade and scraper bowl. Confirm adequate air pressure in all four tires. Check all fluid levels.
2. Climb into operator's seat. Caution: Do not attempt to start machine if not seated in operator's seat. Machine is not equipped with safety neutral starting switch. It *can* be started in gear. It *can* run over you.
3. Looking at instrument panel, locate engine on-off switch (second from left). Pull it out.
4. If this is the first start of day, pull out carburetor choke (second from right).
5. Locate engine electrical starting switch (far left). Pull it out and hold it until engine starts and runs.
6. Once engine starts, release starting switch, push in choke knob and slightly depress foot accelerator.
7. Observe all four instrument gauges to confirm proper electrical system charging by amp gauge, confirm adequate oil pressure, monitor water temperature gauge, and observe the engine hours meter.
8. Once engine reaches operating temperature, use bulldozer blade control lever to raise blade off ground; use bowl control lever to raise scraper off ground. Depress clutch. Select either first gear for forward or reverse gear as required. Release clutch smoothly, proceed cautiously.

Warning: If you are under hostile fire, ignore all above instructions. Jump into scraper bowl and prepare to kiss your tail goodbye.

the opportunity to introduce his products to the Midwest and the East Coast contractors.

"You see, Caterpillar built only the tractor then," Peterson continued. "LeTourneau built the power control unit, the bulldozer, the scrapers, everything else.

"Caterpillar was on the other side of the river. They were in East Peoria, we were in Peoria itself. And they would start a railroad car with a tractor and ship it over to us. We had a spur right into our building. We'd mount the dozer and the power control unit and put the scraper on the same car, turn it lose, and she'd go to the destination. It worked out beautifully."

In Peoria, LeTourneau again attacked the idea of self-powered scrapers. With rubber tires, his scrapers could move faster when they were loaded than the Caterpillar crawlers that towed them could travel. In fact, their speed was limited only by what the steel-track crawlers could do. With his own staff of engineers by this time, LeTourneau began to conceive and design again.

"'Where's the rest of it?' was a question I was asked so often that I came to admire my own patience in not blowing up," LeTourneau reminisced in his autobiography. "My stock answer was, 'What more do you want?' but it

1953 Caterpillar D4

Above, the four-cylinder 4.50x5.50in diesel engine produced 39.4 drawbar horsepower at 1400rpm. The D4 weighs 11,175lb and in its 1955 Nebraska tests it pulled 9,976lb in first gear. A five-speed transmission provided a top speed of 5.4mph. Dick Akin owns this crawler.

1953 Caterpillar D4
and 1936 Model RD4

Left, Dick Akin's 1953 D4 moves dirt at a reservoir using his brother Ed's LeTourneau Model D scraper. Wayne Swart's 1936 RD4 with its LeTourneau bulldozer blade waits to assist with a push as the scraper bucket fills.

didn't seem very satisfactory. Everybody knew that a tractor had to have four wheels or a whole series of wheels supporting a track-type tread. A machine with no front wheels just didn't make sense to anybody.

"The Tournapull that I designed in 1937 was a thing of beauty only when it tore into action. Otherwise, it looked so ridiculous that tractor manufacturers could not believe I was serious in suggesting that it would one day replace their machines. It had a square, ugly snout housing a Diesel engine, a driver's seat, and two huge rubber tire wheels. That was all."

It was another LeTourneau creation from a mind never made patient or satisfied by past activities.

A sign R. G. Le Tourneau saw in a machine shop were he once worked read: "Where did you get your good judgment? From my experience. And where did you get your experience? From my bad judgement." A superficial reading of LeTourneau's autobiography would suggest that he never had bad judgment or bad luck. In fact, his book is filled with tales of the opposite kind of experiences, all of which tempered his judgment but did little to contain his creativity.

"I miscalculated often, learning by doing so, and only once was it serious." He had been hired to clear a large field of tree stumps, and was using a stationary engine with cables and pulleys to reach out far from the engine. "I had cleared all the stumps within 300 yards and was really reaching out for the rest. I put power to the cable drum. The cable had that warning hum, and I glanced up at the spar tree to see if it would topple under the load. Boing!

"[You] hear that 'boing' sound on television as a gag, but that was the sound I heard and it was no gag. Before I could twist my upturned face away, the snapped cable dropped across my mouth. Like that, half my front teeth were gone. Yards of falling cable wrapped around me like wet string. By the time I untangled myself, and dusted myself off, and discovered I was still alive, I was beginning to get the idea that on hazardous jobs in the wilderness, a man ought to have a partner. There'd be somebody to tell the others how you had been killed, and maybe save them from [making] the same mistake."

Chapter 12

Overhead Reflux, Fractions, and Shaved Heads

Liquified Petroleum Gas Tractors ◆ Propane and Butane Conversions ◆
Distilling Fuels ◆ A Time of Boom and Bust ◆ Hot-Rodded Caterpillars

*F*ortune magazine wrote in 1948 about the vaporization-like expansion of the butane and propane business during the preceding fifteen years. The magazine likened it to: "a surge of thousands of rugged little entrepreneurs with a truck and a couple of hundred dollars in the bank, peddling gas and appliances from back door to back door. It was difficult to fail. Most did well; several piled up fortunes. It was big business to these little go-getters, but small potatoes to the producers—just a by-product and not very exciting at that."

Liquified petroleum gas—LPG—was a waste gas. Before its commercial value as propane and butane was recognized, it was derisively known as "wet gas," "greased air," "fizz gas," and "overhead reflux." Once a market was conceived for it, however, it was proudly—and profitably—sold as Gasol and Gasolite, Pyrofax and Pyrogene, Readygas and Flamo, Skelgas, Shellane, Bu-Gas, and finally as propane and butane.

It had been "discovered" in 1912 by a thirty-one-year-old consulting chemist, Dr. William O. Snelling, while working for the US Geological Survey Explosives Laboratory in Washington, D. C. Snelling succeeded in liquefying natural gas and storing it in a thick glass bowl. He lit the vapor above the liquid and used it to light his office for months before ever saying a word about it to anyone. He described the gas to William Altdorfer, an *Indianapolis Star* writer: "The gas is prepared from 'heavy' natural gas, particularly waste gas which accumulates in the pipes of oil wells. The natural gas is compressed and cooled, and the heavy fractions which condense are separated. The lighter fractions are next condensed and are forced under pressure into a vessel called the 'rectifier,' where they come in contact with coils of super-heated steam and are completely vaporized. The gases then pass in succession through a series of coils, each heated to a lower temperature than the preceding one, and these coils separate the gas into a series of products. The higher compounds of the paraffin series of hydrocarbons—to which the chemical names of 'ethane,' 'propane,' and 'butane' have been given—are liquified."

In chemical terms, "fractioning" refers to separating the various elements of any mixture by distillation or crystalization. The success of this process relies on the fact that each element has a different boiling point or solubility that it allows to be separated from other elements.

It began with the Germans as early as 1860, when Julius Pintsch, developed a compressed gas for high-temperature oil processes. His discovery was followed in fifty years with the invention of a process to liquify petroleum gas by another German chemist, Hermann Blau. Patented in the United States in 1904, Blau gas had a foul aroma, but it was used as cooking and lighting fuel, and Blau's patent covered bottling it for mass distribution so that it could be sold in food stores.

Between 1905 and 1910, several LPG pioneers established businesses to deal with separating, storing, and marketing the wet, greasy gases. Frank Peterson in Mercer, Pennsylvania, in 1905 extracted gas from anthracite coal, which he then used as fuel for his own small engines. In 1909, Andy and Chester Kerr formed Riverside Oil Company in Pittsburgh to produce natural gas. In the next two years, Riverside built twenty gas plants and launched the boom. In 1912, more than 1,000 new plants opened in western Pennsylvania and Virginia.

Robert Clay, managing editor of the *Butane-Propane News*, authored a fifty-year history of the industry in 1962. His own prose was colorful, and his interview with Andy Kerr was entertaining. Clay set the scene as it was in the early days: "The gasoline obtained from these plants was an ornery, dangerous product. It contained a considerable volume of petroleum gases that boiled out of the liquid, whether it was in storage, in transit, or in use. Andy Kerr once rather colorfully and modestly described his side of this situation, 'I deserve no credit for being the first to plunge into the sale of butane and propane. I tried in every way to avoid selling these products. I tried to pass them on to the gasoline trade, but they boiled out of our casing-head

1932 Caterpillar Model 60
Above, in the early 1950s, six ex-Panama Canal Model 60s were converted to propane fuel and used in Orange County, California.

1927 Caterpillar Model 60 Butane with Harris Harvester
Opposite page, David Sanders of Durham, California, still uses his Model 60.

1927 Caterpillar Model 60 Butane with Harris Harvester

Alex Giusti of Yuba City, California, checks his rice crop before beginning to cut. As short as harvest days are, the overnight dew must dry before the raw grain can be taken. Behind him, his George H. Harris rice harvester waits.

gasoline and splashed red ink all over our ledger. These liquid gases made our works at Sistersville so dangerous that we were compelled to build high waste lines with Christmas tree outlets [dump and drainage lines that spread out like the branches of a tree] in order to avoid having an excess of dangerous gas float over the Baltimore & Ohio Railroad main line adjoining the works. I was literally forced to put this gas in its proper place. A daily loss of 1400gal [of vaporized gases] at that time amounted to approximately $150, and no Scotchman could overlook that.'"

Capturing and controlling the vapor was where its orneriness and the danger came in. Herman Stukeman, one of Andy Kerr's young engineers, filed a report on the Kerrs' Riverside efforts on Christmas Eve 1910: "While we were condensing the first liquid, our gas line broke and filled the room to a depth of 1ft with gas. Apparently, the gas did not have enough air mixed with it to burn, except above the 1ft-depth. Two helpers in the engine room—who, as helpers will, were watching the boss repair the leak—had rings burned around their trousers 1ft from the floor; otherwise, they were untouched.

"The supervisor [Andy Kerr], being in the fire zone and on his knees, had within the week a new and thinner skin on

his face and hands. On retiring from the room, as all did promptly, the gas was observed to be burning from the top, about 12in from the floor. No harm was done, except to the complexion. After our fire experience, we had considerable respect for this gas. [From then on,] we used welded containers and gas regulators and reduced the gas to low pressures."

Independently—and in much greater safety—Snelling had determined scientifically what Andy Kerr had learned painfully: Liquified petroleum gas was a mixture of propane, butane, pentane, and other separated gas mixture elements.

Still, the dangers were not past. A few months later, one of Kerr's employees at the Sistersville plant was frozen by escaping butane and died. Through fire and ice, each passing horror expanded the body of knowledge. Snelling joined the Kerrs in late 1911, and together they founded American Gasol, the name Chester Kerr had given to the propane fraction a year before. And two years later, they were all bought out by the founder of America's most successful home study programs, LaSalle Extension Course. E. W. De-Bower had done his homework, learning a great deal about the economic potential of the gases. He offered the partners $50,000 for their company, and all but Snelling were glad to be out of the risky—if suddenly profitable—business.

Development continued. During World War I, Dr. J. B. Garner of Hope Natural Gas Company in Pittsburgh introduced the word "butane" to consumers. Garner worked to improve its image. Nicknamed "greasy air," the gas had been previously promoted for industrial uses; some thought it was still too risky for home use, even though butane had successfully powered an automobile in 1912. But by 1920, the Kerrs, back in the business again, had concluded that greasy air would " work very well in practically any gasoline-type burner." In 1922, LPG sales totalled 223,000gal nationwide. And from the beginning, the Kerr brothers sparked LPG's next big flash.

Andy Kerr moved to Long Beach, California, and set up the Imperial Gas Company in 1925. As he explained later to Robert Clay, "It was thought that the Imperial Valley [a desert farming area between Indio and El Centro] would be a good market. The first set—a recarburetting kind of wet gas outfit—was too expensive, as it consisted of two regulators, one of which used liquid, and it had three tanks. While this plant would use any type of cheap product, it sold for $125." That was not cheap in 1925.

When Kerr concluded that this was far too costly for the California farmers, he simplified the package into the first successful tank-vapor system using one tank and one

1927 Caterpillar Model 60 Butane with Harris Harvester

In the early 1930s, many farmers in California converted their gas-engine Cat 60s to butane fuel. Gas cost 16–18¢ a gallon whereas butane was available for 4–5¢.

1927 Caterpillar Model 60 Butane

with Harris Harvester

Old Caterpillars do not die; the yellow
paint just falls off. David Sanders still
uses his converted Model 60 on his
farm. When butane became hard to
obtain, Sander's father, Lloyd,
converted again—this time to propane.

regulator. This was intended for home heating and cooking, and Kerr was assisted by both Standard Oil Company of California and Shell Oil Company, which was poised to introduce its own propane-propylene mixture, Shellane. Standard's Long Beach-based Lomita Oil Company soon brought out Readygas, which it test marketed and introduced as Flamo. And Phillips Petroleum, then the largest natural gas producer, began to examine the challenges, logistics, and value in transporting liquified petroleum gases by rail to distributors around the United States. As home owners in rural areas began to accept butane and propane for home heating and cooking uses, the manufacturers continued working out the kinks in the hardware.

Clay described an ongoing struggle: "It was not uncommon for domestic sets to lose many pounds of fuel each day. Because LPG not only operated under higher pressure, but also had pronounced solvent qualities, the loose fits, rubber compounds, and grease packing that worked with natural gas would not work very long with LPG." Yet even as the chemists and researchers, tinkerers and inventors struggled with these problems, other individuals sought new uses for the fuels.

Standard Oil had established Lomita Oil in 1923,

pumping gas and fractioning it from its pumps and fields on Signal Hill at the north end of the city of Long Beach. Sometime in 1928, as Lomita was beginning to promote the commercial uses of propane and butane, Charles McCartney, a Stanford University engineering dropout, walked in the front door with an idea. McCartney believed either of the two gases could be used as motor fuels. He asked Lomita to put him in business distributing gas for this virtually untapped market. He quickly founded Petrolane and began selling butane as an engine fuel to farmers from El Centro to Bakersfield.

At that time, in 1928, Los Angeles-based George Holzapfel—among others—had begun work to develop LPG carburetors. A year later, Shell had a truck in its fleet testing the fuel on a daily basis. In 1930, due in part to McCartney's vision, Standard of California announced that 127 of its salesmen would be driving its Flamo-powered trucks. And, as Clay pointed out, Flamo was propane, and the large Standard Oil program produced a huge butane by-product surplus.

This was, of course, a time of boom and bust. McCartney was selling a conversion that cost $150–$250 for a farm tractor. But once converted, the tractor ran on fuel that cost

4–5¢ per gallon compared to 18¢ for gasoline. In addition, butane burned so much cleaner that routine maintenance such as oil changes could be stretched to nearly double the engine running time. Furthermore, as a fuel, butane simply produced more power than gasoline. Other inventors and manufacturers joined as outside suppliers to the volatile market. Still others enlisted as inventors-turned-disciples.

Roy Hansen, a licensed mechanical and civil engineer in Lomita, was in business manufacturing carburetors and tanks in 1933. He formed an alliance with Petrolane, and Hansen and McCartney began traveling north to Stockton and Sacramento and beyond in search of new customers and new distributors. In early 1933, McCartney established Lloyd McClure in Bakersfield and the Winther Brothers in Fresno as sales and installation outposts as LPG spread north. In late 1933, Hansen met Lewis Dunning and his twenty-seven-year-old son Albert Dunning north of Sacramento. Lewis Dunning had been the business end of Dunning-Erich Harvesters, which became the Harrington Harvesters.

Lewis and Albert Dunning also raised grain and rice around Knights Landing, north of Sacramento. Lewis sold the virtues of butane fuel to Steve Detling, a neighbor with

1927 Caterpillar Model 60 Butane with Harris Harvester

The Harris harvester "bridge" even has a ship-like wheel. It controls the 24ft-long header while the LPG Cat 60 pulls and steers the Harris Harvester around the rice field.

1928 Caterpillar Model 30 Butane

Right, Robert Stanghellini converted his 1928 Model 30 to butane in the early 1930s. The 175psi large tank fed through a regulator mounted at the rear of the Caterpillar four-cylinder engine. The Ensign carburetor was also modified.

1932 Caterpillar Model 60

Lower left, restored and owned by Virgil Chritton of Pomona, California, this crawler regularly performs demonstrations and displays around southern California. Butane and propane conversions were popular in the 1930s.

1928 Caterpillar Model 30 Butane

Lower right, to convert Model 30s to butane, the process differed only one way from work done to Model 60s. Owners shaved the larger tractors' cylinder heads up to 0.75in. The smaller crawlers left the cylinder heads untouched but replaced stock pistons with high-compression versions.

1932 Caterpillar Model 60

Opposite page, even in the 1930s, the Panama Canal was still work in progress. Six Model 60s worked for about ten years on road construction and repair as well as shoreline renovation and reconstruction.

a Caterpillar 60. Hansen came with his carburetor on November 23, 1933, supervised the installation, and by the end of the day, the Dunnings were in a new business.

"The advantage over gasoline was that you still got the power—more power—on butane," Albert Dunning explained. "The per-gallon consumption was just about the same. But what you also got was the substantial cost reduction. You saved more than half the price of gasoline. We took the gasoline tank off and fitted a 60gal butane tank. These tanks were much heavier and contained a safety valve set at about 175psi. The regulator was mounted on the carburetor itself; it was called a regulator, or vaporizer.

"The liquid fuel was ice cold. It had to be heated to make it vaporize. Starting the 60, the motor had to run on vapor out of the top of the tank for about ten minutes. It took about this long to warm up the motor before it would have hot water to run through the regulator in order to heat the fuel.

"They couldn't run the tractor very long on vapor," Dunning said, "because the lean mixture would burn the valves. So after the motor got hot, the vapor valve was turned off and the liquid valve was turned on. The regulator would vaporize the fuel before it got to the carburetor. On the Hansen, Roy drilled into the side of the carburetor underneath the venturi and tapped in a 3/8in pipe fitting. Then a hose was run from the regulator to the carburetor and the fuel adjustments made off the regulator."

Albert Dunning became not only salesman and installer but also made service calls and hauled fuel. To serve the farmer, Dunning had a 3000gal storage tank installed near his home. Each of the farmers was sold a 250 or even a 1000gal tank, and Dunning ran delivery routes all day—and all night long during harvest season. His wife Eleanor became adept at overhauling regulators on the kitchen table when farmers arrived unannounced with problems and Albert was out on his rounds.

Engine conversion from running on gasoline to butane required not only modifying the carburetor and adding a regulator to reduce the tank's high pressure and cold temperature to combustible levels. It needed one additional change: Engine compression needed to be increased. For this reason, most conversions were sold most easily and accomplished most effectively when the tractor was down for an overhaul. Gasoline at that time rated 61 octane, whereas butane rated 93 and propane was 125. The higher compression in the engine was necessary to avoid "pinging," a pre-ignition detonation of the fuel which could burn valves and burn holes in pistons. Under normal practices, Dunning explained, they put in high-rise pistons on Caterpillar 30s, and on the 60s, they shaved the cylinder heads 3/4in. But farmers have always been tinkerers and some of those tinkerers fancied themselves as hot-rodders too. "What if" became a question that was never asked of the people who already knew the answers.

"If you weren't very careful," Dunning began, "as to how much to grind off the heads, the rocker arms would collide inside your engine and raise heck. We got away from that. Sometimes when these fellows did too much, they couldn't even turn the engine over with a cranking bar. So one guy,

1927 Caterpillar Model 60 Butane with Harris Harvester
Alex Giusti waits at the end of the balance beam for sunrise and his harvest crew. Normally, Giusti uses modern equipment for the harvest. A chance to relive his grandfather's experiences was an abnormal opportunity.

1932 Caterpillar

Model 65 Butane conversion

Above, this 65 has an on-board hydraulic system produced by Be-Ge Manufacturing Co. of Gilroy, California. This used a pump driven off the final driveshaft, below the reservoir mounted behind the operator's head. Alongside the operator was the 175psi-rated steel butane tank.

1932 Caterpillar

Model 65 Butane conversion

Opposite page, like many crawlers in California, this Model 65—Caterpillar's largest at the time—was converted to butane. In Nebraska tests, the 7.00x8.50in bore-and-stroke engine produced 54 drawbar and 78.4 brake horsepower at 650rpm on gas.

Starting the Caterpillar Model 60 with Butane

In the old days, the tractor was run on butane using a 125psi tank. Now that butane is very difficult to obtain, most owners have converted to propane, which requires a 250psi tank. Starting procedures are unchanged.

1. Walk around the tractor, checking for leaks and frayed or broken cables on the winch or bulldozer.
2. Service the tracks daily. Grease them with a track grease gun.
3. Once a week, service the final drive, and check the rear end and transmission.
4. Check the oil and water.
5. Fuel the tractor from the farm LPG storage tank.
6. Check to make certain the transmission is in neutral.
7. If there is a winch or dozer blade, make sure the master clutch is released. Sometimes these clutches rust and stick.
8. Open the throttle one-quarter.
9. Pour about 1/2oz of gasoline into each priming cock on the intake manifold.
10. Release the compression on the cylinder barrels.
11. Crack open the vapor valve for a fraction of a second to charge the propane regulator and carburetor so there is no lag when the engine starts.
12. Using the starting bar, roll the flywheel up around up to the magneto mark, where the pistons are coming up on compression past the compression release cocks. Then reach over to one or two holes—as far as you can—with the bar. Give it a big pull and see what happens.
13. Repeat the procedure on the flywheel until it starts.
14. As soon as it starts, open the vapor value immediately. Let it run on vapor until the engine warms up, usually 5–10 minutes.
15. Switch over to liquid fuel by opening the liquid valve and closing the vapor valve.

Note: Some of the Ensign carburetors could be set up on "choke" position for starting. But the carburetor must be in excellent condition for this to work. Starting it on gasoline is much easier. If the carburetor is in good shape, set it on "choke," turn on the vapor valve, and start cranking the engine. It should start.

---

he got smart. Thinking that since we got by with 3/4in, he'd just go 7/8in." Dunning shook his head in sympathy, but a broad smile betrayed him. "And that was just a little bit too much. Because when he got to cranking it, he couldn't turn it over. He had to get another Caterpillar out in front of him to pull him to get it started. If he killed his engine half a mile out there in the field, he had to go get another tractor and operator to come out and tow him started."

Another farmer whose name Dunning has forgotten to protect him from embarrassment, figured that if shaving the heads of the 60s worked well and if high-compression pistons on the 30s worked well, then using both together would work even better. "He shaved the heads 3/4in [and] installed high-rise pistons, and when they started the tractor up, it ran maybe a few dozen revolutions. It made an awful racket, sounded just like a jackhammer. And then it blew the crankcase studs right out of the block—those studs that held the cylinders to the crankcase. He had to replace the crankcase. He was so embarrassed."

In 1929, LPG sales had reached nearly 10 million gallons; in 1934, 56 million gallons were sold. Farmers in rice and grain country had adapted their driers to butane. Then in 1941, Minneapolis-Moline introduced the first factory-produced LPG tractors.

In a 1935 paper, Hal Higgins outlined the cost reductions available to the farmer through LPG- and Diesel-powered tractors. He reiterated the still-lingering safety concerns of LPG and natural gas, for which regulations were being considered by the state of California: "Hazards due to handling butane often exist but are not apparent. Conditions may be ripe to result in disaster. Since the vapor is colorless and odorless, it may be taken into the lungs of an individual without his knowledge and result in death. Men are trapped by apparent safety."

Initiated by the US Bureau of Mines, testing of odorized gas had begun in the mid-1920s. The Bureau found that no single odor was perfect: Some people had colds, others couldn't smell at all, others didn't notice certain odors." Emerson Thomas, a consulting engineer with Phillips Petroleum, began odorizing Phillips's products before the US regulations. Standard Oil of California tested Thiophane, mixing 6-1/2lb per 10,000gal, but found it unsatisfactory. Chemists throughout the industry tested Ethyl Mercaptain, a substance the *Guinness Book of World Records* calls the "smelliest substance on earth." This is still in use, mixed at 1lb per 10,000gal. It became the US standard, published in US Bureau of Mines "Pamphlet 58" in May 1932.

Still, understanding the properties of the gases led to broader knowledge of the risks and limits and from those, to other possible applications.

Years after one of Andy Kerr's employees froze to death from butane, Albert Dunning used much more carefully controlled doses to rid his childrens' arms and legs of poison oak. A short, quick spray got rid of the inflammation and itching immediately.

A decade after that, when war made gasoline unobtainable, LPG fell first under the jurisdiction of the War Production Board, which didn't limit production but hampered shipments due to the severe railroad tank car shortages. In 1943, the Petroleum Administrator for War took over LPG and the Office of Defense Transportation moved LPG off the rails and onto the highways. By the time it all ended, hundreds of thousands of tractors across the United States were running on LPG. And Hansen and Dunning, McClure, Winther, and McCartney had more than 20,000 tractors running on LPG in the San Joaquin and Sacramento Valleys alone.

Chapter 13

Engineering Challenges

The High Cost of Fuel in Farming and Construction ✦ *Powershift Transmission Development* ✦ *Caterpillar Expands into Construction Equipment* ✦ *Purchase of Russell Grader in 1928* ✦ *Debut of the D10 and D11*

"One-third to one-half the annual cost of owning and operating a tractor is for fuel," according to Howard F. McColly, writing in the US Department of Agriculture 1960 yearbook, *Power to Produce.* In 1959, farmers in the United States used about 250 million gallons of liquified petroleum gas as tractor and truck fuel (and another 65 million gallons in drying and curing crops). A year later, total tractor production just tipped 165,000 machines, with 84,000 operated on gasoline and LPG and 81,000 powered by Diesel engines.

Tractors were designed to run on a variety of fuels, ranging from high-octane gas that provided high performance and maximum efficiency at substantial cost to the lowest-octane, cheapest distillate fuels. Many of these less-expensive, inefficient fuels, such as "stove top," were developed as byproducts of the refining processes, and were made available to farmers for low prices up until World War II. Farmers' costs per acre and contractors' cost per hour were a big concern, even before such figures were as carefully monitored as they are now.

For the engineers who developed the tractors' power-plants—and for the Sales and Marketing Departments attempting to sell small numbers of specific engines in certain markets—the plethora of fuels available to customers created complications. The development time and budgets available to researchers and engineers had to be shared among gasoline-, LPG-, Diesel-, and even kerosene- and distillate-fired engines.

By 1958, seventeen states imposed gasoline taxes, ranging from 4¢ to 7¢ per gallon, which did not exempt off-highway use. A survey in Kansas revealed that a 7¢ gas tax added 77 percent to the cost of plowing over the costs incurred using non-taxed fuels. Thanks to increased popularity of the jet-engine airplane that used kerosene as a fuel, Diesel fuel costs increased to nearly the same level as gasoline. Tractor builders quickly recognized that the Diesel engine's performance and economy made it the obvious choice as the predominant fuel of the future.

Gasoline engines now run at 7:1 or 8:1 compression, while Diesels and LPG engines operate at about 17:1. But the heat output of each fuel—and therefore the amount of work done per gallon—is where the difference shows more clearly. A gallon of butane produces 102,200Btu. (One British thermal unit is the amount of heat required to raise 1lb of water 1deg Fahrenheit.) A gallon of regular-grade gasoline offers 124,300Btu; a gallon of Diesel fuel, 139,000Btu. In the mid-1950s, the cost of Diesel fuel was still less than that of gasoline, and its higher heat value made it more economical. Manufacturers recognized this. In 1952, Minneapolis Moline introduced Diesel engines in its Model U tractors, and in 1954, Deere offered its first Diesel engines for the 70 series tractors. By 1975, when US tractor manufacturers produced nearly 194,000 machines, 90 percent—more than 177,000—were powered by a Diesel. The predictions of Henry Kaiser, Oscar Starr, and Art Rosen had come true. And while the engine designers continued to work to produce more power even more smoothly from the Diesel, the rest of Caterpillar's engineers worked equally hard to get that power more efficiently onto the ground.

Through the early 1950s, Caterpillar adopted the wet clutch, or multiple disc clutch, operated in oil. This development noticeably improved clutch life because the oil served as a coolant and reduced the damaging effects of friction while allowing the driving- and driven-plates to be engaged more effectively.

Turbochargers appeared on Caterpillar crawlers in late 1953 and throughout 1954 as company engineers field-tested a new model in construction, logging, and pipe-laying. When the nearly 18ft-long, 56,000lb, 286hp D9 tractor was introduced in May 1955, it was the world's largest and most powerful production crawler. Its 6.25x8.00in six-cylinder engine produced 230hp on the drawbar, and Caterpillar offered an optional three-stage torque-converter transmission.

Then, in October 1959, Caterpillar announced its Powershift transmission that combined through planetary

1984 Caterpillar Model D10

Above, there were 46 sealed and lubricated tracks per side. The Powershift transmission provided a top speed forward of 7.2mph.

1974 Caterpillar D8H

Opposite page, the seven track rollers put 10ft of 22in-wide sealed tracks on the ground on each side.

1937 Caterpillar Model D6
with Deere Model 36 Harvester
In 1935, Deere & Co. sold Caterpillar
products as did Caterpillar to customers
needing wheel tractors. When the
agreement dissolved, the Western
Harvester subsidiary was sold to Deere
and one of its successful products became
the John Deere Model 36 harvester.

gears a blend of the direct-drive power tractor operators knew and torque-converter smoothness. Driven through the D8 or D9 Diesel engine's flywheel, Powershift split one-third of the engine torque to the transmission input shaft, while the other two-thirds ran through the torque converter. Powershift eliminated the flywheel clutch lever, the gearshift lever, and the forward and reverse levers inside the operator's cab. Gears could be shifted on the fly even with the tractor fully load thanks to a direct-acting hydraulic control, which engaged the speed gear first and then engaged the forward or reverse gear selector. This allowed the operator to use the engine and transmission to best tailor the power and torque to the load at any given moment.

Beginning in 1957, thirty test D8 and D9 tractors were equipped with Powershift. Through years of testing in the fields, in mines, on construction jobs, and at logging sites, these machines accumulated more than 50,000 hours of evaluation and development time before their production was announced.

Western wheat and grain farmers were always treated well and their product needs attended to by Caterpillar and by Best and Holt before the 1925 consolidation. In 1926, Caterpillar organized the Western Harvester Company as a wholly owned subsidiary to take over the operation of the Holt Harvester Works. In 1930, this was sold, and 13 1/2 acres were added to the Peoria works for harvester manufacturing. Then in 1935, this entire operation was sold to Deere & Company in exchange for marketing and sales agreements that offered Caterpillar showroom exposure for its crawlers in Deere stores throughout the world.

Soon after Thomas Baxter assumed presidency of the Holt Company following Benjamin Holt's death in 1920, Caterpillar began a vigorous expansion into road construction. From the earliest days of Holt Caterpillars and Best Tracklayers, the products of the Russell Grader Manufacturing Company of Minneapolis had been a familiar sight as they were towed behind thecrawlers. Founded in 1903, Russell Grader was one of the first to develop blade-type and elevating road graders. It produced modifications to pair a Holt two-ton tractor with the rear of its grader, fitting it as the rear drive unit for its early Self-Propelled Motor Patrols.

**1937 Caterpillar Model D6
with Deere Model 36 Harvester**
Right, rice paddies are drained a week
before harvest to dry the ground. Once
the morning dew burns off, harvesting
begins. At sunrise, the 1947 harvester
dwarf's Ross Willey's 1937 D6.

**1937 Caterpillar Model D6
with Deere Model 36 Harvester**
Below, the dry ground easily supports
a heavy crawler and harvester. But
crawlers are essential if harvest must
occur right after rain. The D6 weighs
17,750lb and can pull 16,674lb in
first gear.

1939 Caterpillar Model D5

The 1939 Model D5 used the detuned engine from the D6 mounted on the chassis of the D4. Only 45 were built, primarily for military use, until the model designation was resurrected in the mid-1960s.

Starting the Caterpillar D8-2U Series Tractor

1. Before attempting to start the starting engine, check the Diesel engine and tractor controls, as well as the starting engine controls, to see that they are in the corret position for starting.

Note: Be sure to check the crankcase oil level of the Diesel engine and the starting engine to make certain that the oil is up to the full mark on the gauge.

2. Disengage the flywheel clutch by pushing it all the way forward. Place the forward-reverse lever in neutral.

3. Shift the speed selector lever in to neutral.

4. Move the fuel injection pump control lever to the extreme forward position with the plunger at the back of the stop so that the injection pumps are closed.

5. Set the starting engine transmission control lever in the "high" speed position.

6. Move the compression release lever to the "start" position.

7. Disengage the starting engine clutch by pushing the lever in toward the Diesel engine block.

8. Open the starting engine fuel valve by unscrewing the fuel valve control. Pull out the starting engine choke control rod.

9. Move the idling latch to hold the starting engine governor lever in the idling position.

10. Turn on the ignition switch.

11. If the engine is cold, advance the spark; if warm, retard the spark.

12. Insert the crank in position and crank until the engine starts.

13. When the engine starts, keep the speed low until the crankcase lubricating oil has a chance to warm up and better lubricate the engine.

14. Check to see that the starting engine clutch and flywheel clutch are disengaged.

15. Check to see that the starting engine is running at idling speed.

16. Apply the starting engine clutch brake to stop the starter pinion from rotating by pushing the clutch control lever all the way in toward the Diesel engine and holding it there.

17. Engage the starter pinion with the flywheel ring gear by pulling out on the starter pinion control lever; then release the clutch brake and partially engage the clutch to be sure the starter pinion has been fully engaged.

18. Push in the choke control.

19. Release the idling latch to let the starting engine run at its full governed speed. Engage the starting engine clutch by pulling out the lever as far as possible. If the engine slows to the stalling point when the clutch is engaged, as it might in cold weather, disengage the clutch and let the engine speed up again.

20. Move the compression release lever to the "run" position as soon as the starting engine is cranking the Diesel engine at normal cranking speed.

Note: The heat generated when the starting engine is cranking the Diesel engine against compression and the circulation of the starting engine exhaust through the tube in the Diesel engine inlet warms the cylinders, pistons, and combustion chambers to the starting temperature.

21. After the starting engine has cranked the Diesel engine against compression until the Diesel is sufficiently warm, pull out the plunger and move the fuel injection pump control lever back to approximately half the engine speed position.

22. When the Diesel engine begins to run, the starter pinion disengages automatically, but it is necessary to disengage the starting engine clutch by pushing the clutch control lever in toward the engine.

23. Stop the starting engine by closing the valve at the carburetor, allowing the engine to burn all the fuel in the carburetor. Then turn off the ignition switch.

24. Allow the Diesel engine to idle 5 minutes with the fuel injection pump control lever to half the engine speed position before applying load. Normal oil pressure should register around 30psi on the gauge when running at rated speed and lower at idle. If no pressure is indicated, investigate immediately.

25. Once a normal operating temperature—170deg Fahrenheit— is reached, begin to work.

In 1928, Caterpillar purchased Russell Grader, and in 1931, the aging Motor Patrol was replaced with Caterpillar's new Auto Patrol. This was a single-piece machine that integrated the wheel-type power unit with the flexibility and adaptability of the elevating blade-type graders. Its Caterpillar name at first confused salesmen. When first shown photographs of the new product, many demanded reassurance from the company that the Auto Patrol would indeed be a crawler track-drive machine. But Caterpillar engineers were aware of the developments that Le-Tourneau, their collaborator across the river, had made with rubber-wheel scrapers. The salesmen told the branch personnel what they wanted to hear, and the engineers produced what they knew the contractors wanted to buy.

World War II brought new requirements for materiel and new opportunities for the company. Caterpillar produced an unbeatable crawler transmission. Civilian tractor production was reduced. Factory floor space was devoted to producing military machinery, including tank transmissions, howitzer carriages, and even artillery shell casings. The Caterpillar Military Engine Company was established in Decatur, Illinois, to produce radial air-cooled Diesel engines for tanks. And an agreement was made with American Car and Foundry Company in Berwick, Pennsylvania, to assemble under license nearly 1,100 olive-drab green D7 crawlers to military specifications each month. In addition, Caterpillar began producing stationary power units and electricity-generating sets that incorporated the company's Diesel engines; these were assembled in a package suitable for wartime field use and were strong enough to be parachute-dropped.

Few of the post-World War I doldrums that had plagued Best and Holt materialized after World War II. Caterpillar expanded its production, facilities, and product

1937 Caterpillar Model D6 with Deere Model 36 Harvester

Right, the six-cylinder 4.25x5.50in diesel produced 78 belt horsepower at peak performance, yet returned 13.72hp-hours per gallon of fuel used. Top speed in fifth gear was 5.8mph.

1939 Caterpillar Model D5

Below, available 44in or 60in track gauge, the 11,230lb crawler (1,035lb more than a D4) was Caterpillar's first crawler to pull more than its own weight: 11,300lb in first gear. Paul Kirsch restored and owns this 28th D5 built.

1945 Caterpillar

Model D2 with Traxcavator

Right, the D2 was introduced in 1938 with a 40in or 50in track gauge. Both used the D-3400 3.75x5.00in four-cylinder diesel, producing 25.2 drawbar and 29.98 belt horsepower at 1525rpm.

1945 Caterpillar

Model D2 with Traxcavator

Below, Don Hunter's 9ft-long D2 is dwarfed by the Trackson Model T-2 Traxcavator front-end loader shovel fitted to it. The Traxcavator worked by cables run off the belt pulley to raise the bucket and relied on gravity to lower it.

line. By the end of 1951, nearly 3 million square feet of factory floor space had been added to plants in Peoria, Joliet (for manufacture of LeTourneau-inspired products, such as bulldozers, wheeled self-propelled scrapers, and power control units), and York, Pennsylvania (a track and track roller manufacturing plant specifically located for East Coast and European export markets). In mid-December 1951, Caterpillar acquired the Trackson Company in Milwaukee. Trackson manufactured side-boom pipeline-laying equipment and cable-operated, front-mounted scoop shovels.

The agriculture industry was peculiar in the western United States. At a time when many manufacturers were developing smaller tractors of greater versatility, the western farmer with his vast acreage still needed big tractor power, pure and simple. Caterpillar's products from the 1930s through the 1950s continued to serve the western farmer, but the company's orientation had gone more and more toward broader uses, particularly into construction.

Company management and engineering recognized that shift. In 1966, Caterpillar introduced the first of the SA—Special Application—tractors produced in D4, D5, and D6 versions and engineered for drawbar work. Providing horsepower ranges of 68hp to 125hp, the SA tractors boasted half the ground pressure of comparable weight and similar horsepower wheel tractors. Caterpillar shifted the

engines forward to provide better balance on the tracks. These engines were slightly modified to provide from 20 to nearly 30 percent more torque as well.

Direct-drive transmissions were used. This traded the benefits of Powershift—smooth shifting into a better engine speed range for a momentary heavy load—for more speeds as it was recognized that the SA tractors would be working under a nearly constant load at a set ground speed. Full-length fenders decreased the amount of dust, and padded seats slightly eased the 23hr days so familiar to farmers. An optional toolbar allowed Caterpillar's SA tractors to perform any function provided by any wheeled competitor.

The next major improvement in this application came with the Variable Horsepower feature. In third, fourth, and fifth gears, the D4E SA, D5B SA, and D6D SA boasted nearly 35 percent more horsepower than was available in first and second gears. This was accomplished through an electric switch mounted on the transmission and activating a solenoid—hydraulically repositioning a rack-stop on the governor in the fuel system and allowing more fuel to be injected to increase power. (This was essentially a factory-

1939 Caterpillar Model D5

Above, the 4.25x5.50in bore-and-stroke six-cylinder diesel produced a maximum of 45 drawbar and 52 flywheel horsepower at 1400rpm. It was equipped with the five-speed transmission providing 5.4mph top speed.

1945 Caterpillar D8 with Brush Rake

Left, Caterpillar's D8-8R series with the D-13000 engine was produced from 1941 through 1946. This second series of D8s was rated at 113 drawbar horsepower at 1000rpm, enough to force a brush rake through scrub brush and trees.

1954 Caterpillar D8 and Sheep's-Foot

Right, the D8-13A series provided 155 drawbar horsepower and weighed 39,060lb. LeTourneau's two-section sheep's-foot roller weighed 4,640lb empty and another 4,000lb more when filled with water. Each section was 4ft wide with feet 7in long. It sold new for $850 in 1952.

1954 Caterpillar D8

Middle left, the D8 is 16ft-1in long, 7ft-2in tall, 8ft-8in wide, and at its Nebraska tests, weighed 36,915lb.

1954 Caterpillar D8

Lower right, the 13A series operated at 78in track gauge. Standard track shoes were 22in wide with 8ft-4in of track on the ground. The crawler weight was spread over 30.48sq-ft giving actual ground pressure of 8.4psi.

1954 Caterpillar D8

Below, output from the 5.75x8.00in diesel was beyond Nebraska's ability to measure belt horsepower on its existing dynamometer.

produced electrical-hydraulic high-tech equivalent of having Diesel engineer Art Rosen along on each job. Engaging third, fourth, or fifth gear accomplished something similar to Rosen's "original sin of opening the smoke screw" to increase the power.)

Variable Horsepower was developed and introduced to assist farmers in tillage operations performed at speeds faster than 3 1/2–4mph. This large power increase enabled farmers to perform more work each day, cutting the per

acre costs due to reducing operator hours per acre.

In 1976, Caterpillar introduced its sealed and lubricated tracks. This development completely removed the track pin from the dirt and moisture that caused wear and disintegration. The pin was now surrounded with a lubricant held in place by polyurethane seals, rubber load rings, and a thrust ring. Each track pin contained its own lubricant reservoir as well, and this lubricant eliminated the internal bushing wear. This not only greatly reduced track wear and

1954 Caterpillar D8

The 13A series was produced from 1953 through 1955 and was Caterpillar's most powerful crawler. At 1200rpm, Cat rated the engine at 150 drawbar and 185 belt horsepower.

1954 Caterpillar D8

Sitting near the end of an abandoned airstrip, Ed Akin's D8-13A may have its work cut out for it—literally—between the trees. Akin, a retired airline captain, has a few ideas.

1958 Caterpillar

Model 12 Motorgrader

With its standard 12ft blade, the

Motorgrader weighed 22,410lb.

maintenance costs for the undercarriage, it allowed the development and introduction of the High Drive technology.

By elevating the final drive, Caterpillar reduced several wear-inducing conditions. The drive sprockets were now separated from the track roller frame. With these sprockets containing the steering clutches, brakes, and final drive assemblies, their elevated position allowed the tractor suspension to absorb the direct ground shocks, avoiding direct impact with this critical mechanism. Any torsional load on the

track frame from bulldozer or drawbar implements was also isolated from the sprocket hub. And the higher position reduced the damaging effects of water, dirt, and debris that became caught between the sprocket teeth and track bushings.

Wes McKeen, a salesman for more than thirty years with Tenco Tractor Company in Sacramento, remembered the first High Drive introduced on the new D10. Caterpillar had brought it out to central California for work on the Malones Dam project in 1975: "Caterpillar engineers spent a great

1955 Caterpillar D8-14A Series

Left, the D8-14A series was the first of the D8s with Caterpillar's new D-342 six-cylinder 5.75x8.00in engine. Output was rated at 191.0 flywheel and 157.6 drawbar horsepower at 1200rpm.

1958 Caterpillar Model 12 Motorgrader

Below, early Caterpillar dealers knew that 2-Ton crawlers powered Russell Road Patrol grader machines. When Caterpillar acquired Russell and showed the first Motorgraders, salesmen panicked. Where were the tracks, they asked?

1974 Caterpillar D8H

Right, Caterpillar's Powershift transmission provided three speeds through a single-stage torque converter. Top speed was 6.5mph. The six-speed transmission provided a maximum 52,410lb drawbar pull in first at 1.6mph.

1974 Caterpillar D8H

Below, fitted with the 8U universal bulldozer blade and the 8D triple shank ripper, this machine was 27ft-7in long. The blade and ripper added another 25,000lb to the weight. It was 11ft-2in to the top of the air conditioner and the tractor with blade was 13ft-9in wide.

deal of time out there because that tractor was in severe rock applications. A number of times, they disassembled and re-assembled the tracks and the rear end on that tractor.

"The hard rock applications would have given the most trouble to the tracks and transmissions and to the undercarriage. That was a tremendous test because when that machine came out, it was much bigger than anything else. When it went into production, it was the biggest crawler tractor built in the world, with 700hp [and] weighing about 200,000lb."

McKeen saw the D10 again at a school Caterpillar put on at Peoria. He reflected back on the technology: "The idea behind it was to try to make a machine that was more easily repairable. It fit right in, because they had come out with the sealed, lubricated tracks—the master link instead of master pins." The serviceability became a major advantage to customers. A major component failure—final drive, steering clutch, differential transmission—would have required removing the swing frame, the entire side of the crawler. This would have resulted in 72–96hr of downtime. Because this was now isolated, these repairs could be done in 8hr.

"That's what really started everything," McKeen said. "That was quite an exciting thing when the D10 came out. The first one sold went into agriculture, believe it or not. [It was] bought by Dave Price down toward Stockton. He used it for 'split plowing,' with a big, long single shank—for deep ripping—for orchards and vineyards."

1980 Caterpillar D9L
With its 9U blade (23.9cu-yd capacity)
and deep ripping single shank (6ft-3in
penetration), the fully equipped D9L
weighed 131,044lb.

1955 Caterpillar D8-14A Series

Ed Akin clears storm-felled trees with his brother's D8-14A series crawler. Tested at Nebraska, the 14A-series tractor weighed 47,335lb and pulled 40,032lb. in first gear. Bare tractors weighed slightly less than 20 tons. Some models, fully equipped with angle-dozer blades, roll-over protection and logging winches, could weigh as much as 30 tons.

1980 Caterpillar D9L

With blade, the D9L tractor was 16ft-4in wide. Despite its size, it looked small compared to a 100cu-yd capacity Lectra Haul dumper.

1986 Caterpillar D8L

Above, each tank carried 600gal of anhydrous ammonia used for pre-planting preparation. The 1200gal supply will cover six miles of field in swatches 32ft wide. In the central California valley working mile sections, each "round" takes 45 minutes. Three rounds means a refill.

1980 Caterpillar D9L

Upper left, the 3412 engine was a 60-degree V-12 of 5.40x6.00in bore and stroke. At 1900rpm, the 1649ci diesel produced 460bhp. Fuel capacity was 255gal. Its Powershift transmission provided 7.7mph forward and 9.6mph in reverse.

1984 Caterpillar Model D10

Left, the engine was Caterpillar's D-348T, a 1786ci V-12 with 5.40x6.50in bore and stroke. At 1800rpm, the twin-turbocharged, four-valve-per-cylinder diesel was rated at 700hp at the flywheel.

1980 Caterpillar D9L

Above, the D9L first appeared in 1980, powered by the new 3412 turbocharged V-12 diesel engine. This high-drive configuration isolated the sprocket from rock impact and lessened the likelihood of water submersion.

1984 Caterpillar Model D10

Upper right, overall width was 12ft while track gauge was 114in. Caterpillar offered optional heaters, air conditioning, onboard fire suppression systems, and tracks 32in wide.

1984 Caterpillar Model D10

Right, the D10's 193,700lb sat on 8,624sq-in of steel track. This next generation of power and its ease of service was made possible by elevated final-drive sprockets.

1993 Caterpillar D11N

Left, with its 11U blade, the D11N was 36ft-8in long, 21ft wide, and 14ft-11in to the top of the rollover protection system above the cab. The 11U blade was 7ft-7in tall and had a capacity of 42.2cu-yd of dirt.

1986 Caterpillar D8L

Below, the D8L used the 1099ci 3408 V-8 diesel. Bore and stroke was 5.40x6.00in and output was 335hp at 1900rpm.

1993 Caterpillar D11N

Caterpillar's single shank for deep ripping penetrated 7ft-2in at maximum depth. As equipped, heading off to rip open California's high desert, it is worth nearly $1 million.

1993 Caterpillar D11N

Left, hydraulics enabled the D11N weight to be useful. Vertical penetration force on the shank was as much as 59,900lb—the equivalent to two and a half Best 110hp steamers—and there is 137,330lb of pryout force available when the shank gets stuck.

1993 Caterpillar D11N

Below, twin turbochargers, intercoolers, four valves per cylinder: the new 2105ci 60-degree V-8 engine with 6.70x7.50in bore and stroke produced 770 flywheel horsepower at 1800rpm. Its total weight was 215,525lb.

Chapter 14

The Ultimate Challenges

The New Generation of Caterpillars ✦ Product Support Saves the Day ✦ Debut of the Challengers ✦ A New Vision of Row-Crop Tractors ✦ "You're Caterpillar, You Don't Back Away From Anything"

Toward the end of the 1970s, one more development came out of Peoria. The company was always good at communicating product information to its dealers and customers. But one particular change happened without announcement. Caterpillar Tractor Company began seeking communication *from* its dealers and customers. This was happening for the first time in many years.

"Nothing gets a manufacturer's attention better than lost sales," Paul Athorp commented. Athorp is the shops and equipment manager for J. G. Boswell Company, a large California cotton grower. Until the late 1970s, taking purchasing dollars elsewhere was about the only method dissatisfied customers had to let Caterpillar know that the tractor manufacturer was not making what they needed.

"Sometime around 1980, we had some difficulty on the performance of the D8 Caterpillars," Athorp explained, "and we made a pretty much wholesale switch to Kamatsu. We had gotten up to twenty-eight Kamatsu tractors. We had some specific complaints about Caterpillar's engines [and] transmissions. We felt the machines weren't performing to our standards. [There was] no response.

"We wanted low ground pressure. We wanted high horsepower-to-weight ratio. We didn't feel that we were making any inroads into making a better tractor. And Kamatsu came along with a tractor—high horsepower—and we felt they had something to offer. The price was great. It was a Model D150, gear drive, a direct competitor of a D8.

"We came to miss the Caterpillar support. Excellent product support! Caterpillar product support means that you just don't have downtime. It is highly unusual to be down more than 48hr from Caterpillar. When we had the Kamatsu tractors and something went down and you had to get parts out of Atlanta, you could wait a week. Ten days. That held some sway.

"Then all [of a] sudden, Caterpillar saw what we were doing and what we wanted. They started coming across with the things that we needed; that was about the time they came out with their variable horsepower D6 SA, and

we tested it and proved to ourselves that this was the type of tractor that we wanted. [It had] a little better weight distribution and wide-track plates. It was attractive to us because we really did miss the product support that Caterpillar has. So we went back to Caterpillar."

And soon afterward, Caterpillar came out to see Athorp. The acreage that Athorp's machines farm require late-winter work in preparation for planting. He knew he couldn't get the tractors in too early because of the moisture in the ground but also he couldn't get in too late. His managers gave him a ten-day window—the "sweet zone" he called it—and this meant that his tractors were the limiting factor. If the ground was dry enough, it would support a heavy D6 or D7 tractor and his operators could pull the tools through it to prepare the seed beds in late February.

"We were looking for a high-speed tractor," Athorp said. "We had been exposed to some high-speed, steel-track tractors—a 34,000lb tractor with a 350hp engine. When you have only a short time to cover a lot of acres, speed is important.

"And then one day, [Caterpillar] came to us and said, 'We're thinking of putting these on rubber tracks.' And we were interested, excited about the concept. A high horsepower-to-weight ratio would give us high speed with enough power and weight to do the job we need to do. And we could road transport them.

"Caterpillar's roots were in agriculture—and in this very valley. Fifteen years ago, we woke up ourselves to the effects of compaction of the soil. We learned that up north of us, the rice growers were putting wide track plates on their tractors. And we tried it and found we could get out into the field a little earlier."

The Caterpillar engineers sat in Athorp's office and asked him and others from Boswell what was important and what the tractor should do. Then they began to hint at their latest idea and what that tractor would be able to do.

A couple of years later, in mid-1983, following many more conversations, a strange-looking D6 arrived at Athorp's shops. Its engine had been shifted nearly 30in forward.

1987 Challenger 65

Above, Challengers were used not only for agriculture but they also groom New York City beaches and pull sleds across Antarctica.

1995 Challenger RowCrop 55

Opposite page, announced in fall 1993, the new RowCrop Challengers took the striking appearance of the first Challengers a step forward. Planned introduction was March 1995 for the Model 35 and 45 and October 1995 for the Model 55.

Challenger Prototype

This Caterpillar D6D was the prototype Challenger. The tractor stopped traffic—and especially police— when it drove along the highways. This prototype was cut up after work was finished. Courtesy Paul Athorp

A cab from another Caterpillar model straddled the gap between where the operator would have sat in the open and where the old instrument panel was now situated since the entire engine compartment was moved so far forward. In place of the front steel idler wheel was a pair of rubber highway truck tires. Hard rubber wheels sat on air-shocked trucks. And a broad rubber track with an aggressive diagonal tread pattern surrounded all the exposed track running gear. Athorp was asked to use it and work it hard. Every week, engineers came out to take notes.

"We had this prototype, this D6 with rubber tracks," Athorp recalled. "It didn't have the ten-speed Powershift that they use in the Challenger now, but it was the belted system. So it would go down the road. Caterpillar was looking for undercarriage durability with that rubber-track

D6. And there was another prototype as well, a D3B with the belts. This was all really just a new adaptation of the work that was done for Martin Marrieta on their Mobile High-Speed Missile Launcher"

As agriculture tractor specialist with Tenco Tractor Company in Sacramento, California, Wes McKeen got involved early with the Challenger project as well. He also noticed the change in communication style between Caterpillar and its customers.

"Caterpillar will have a machine," McKeen said, "and they need to get it tested, and they need a good test. A lot of places they have put machines, the prototypes just get forgotten. People get busy, they don't keep track of [them], they don't keep records. And so when Caterpillar finds a person [who] will do this kind of work, well, guess what?

1987 Challenger 65

Right, track tension was a problem on hills and in tight maneuvering. It was accomplished by nitrogen-boosted tensioning springs that provide 17,000lb of force. An air spring between a door-hinge-type suspension arms supported the tractor.

1987 Challenger 65

Far left, the Challenger 65 was powered by the D-3306 turbocharged and intercooled inline 638ci diesel engine. Bore and stroke was 4.75x6.00in and flywheel horsepower was 271 at 2100rpm.

Caterpillar 30/30 Prototype

Left, the Cat 30/30 was an unproduced prototype. The idea of a cab-forward rubber-track machine was suggested to some large operators to see if there was interest. Apparently this concept was also proposed to the United Nations for NATO as a kind of parachute-drop airfield builder, something like LeTourneau's Tournapull Airborne units.

CAT 30/30
Engineer Support Tractor
Prototype

- **MOBIL-TRAC SYSTEM (MTS)**
  State-of-the-art undercarriage technology provides both on- and off-road mobility by combining the best features of tires and steel track

- **TOTAL SELF-DEPLOYABILITY**
  Sustained travel speeds of over 30 mph eliminates the need for motor transport support

- **DUAL OPERATING MODE**
  Dash mounted control quickly converts 30/30 from work to travel mode to provide optimum performance for mission flexibility

- **AUTOMOTIVE TYPE CONTROLS**
  User friendly control logic reduces training requirements and improves operator efficiency

- **FORWARD OPERATOR'S STATION**
  Excellent visibility for both travel and work

- **HYDROPNEUMATIC SUSPENSION**
  Fully suspended MTS design provides high speed cross-country mobility, lockup allows for a rigid work platform

- **C130 TRANSPORTABLE**
  MTS "rubber track" provides runway protection and drive-on, drive-off capability

- **COMMERCIAL COMPONENTRY**
  70% of the prototype vehicle is commercial production parts to ensure high level of performance and worldwide product support

Optimum Mobility and Self-Deployability
CATERPILLAR

1987 Challenger 65

Below, the 30in-wide belts were driven by a two-piece drive wheel at the rear, connected directly to the output shaft of the final drive. Standard belted track grouser height was 2.5in with 72 chevron pattern grousers per track.

1993 Challenger 70C

Opposite page, the Model 70C was introduced in September 1993 and featured a high-capacity cooling system especially for high-drawbar-pull applications at low speed. It was intended to replace Caterpillar's own D6 steel-track tractors in agricultural and other uses.

"They would rather keep their test work closer to home, but California agriculture is somewhat different from the rest of the world. We do heavier work and we're more influenced by the effects of soil compaction than many wheat or corn growers in the Midwest—although that concern is coming on strong back there now."

The first rubber-belted prototypes appeared in 1982. Caterpillar used primarily a D6D and D3B. For a short time, it also used a D4E, painted red and fitted with odd-looking body panels to confuse unintended observers. Later on, with a series of mechanical prototypes known as the 855X series, each of the six successive test tractors bore closer resemblance to the shape, sound, and performance of the final versions. Caterpillar engineers field-tested these "development mules" not only in central Illinois but also as far away as Minot, North Dakota; Bluetown, Texas; Pullman, Washington; and Gila Bend, Arizona.

These machines were worked hard, in some cases running alongside double-tired, articulated, four-wheel-drive tractors doing the same work. They pulled 16ft plow disks 6in deep in fifth gear, nine-bottom 20in moldboard plows cutting 9in deep in muddy soil run in fourth gear, dragging 18 cubic yard Carryalls scraping 5in deep, and in several trials they ran 36ft field cultivators down into streams, stopped the tractor in water above the track rollers, and then simply pulled effortlessly out of the mud in second

gear. Early versions—855X1, X2, and X3—were tested first with parallel ribbed tracks, but the later efforts—X4, X5, and X6—used the production chevron pattern, and the tractors looked complete in many details except for Caterpillar name badges.

Wes McKeen saw his first rubber-belted D6D in late 1982. Having assisted Peoria's engineers with development testing of the High Drives, they looked for advice concerning where to place their new project. Engineers came and went and after a few years of testing, three pre-production prototypes were distributed. One was made available to McKeen for further development work and a complete shakedown for more than a year.

"They told me what they wanted to do with it," he explained. "They wanted to try laser scraping work. They wanted to try plowing, working in wet grounds. Every kind of application we had in our territory, everything that would be a challenge, [or] questionable. The particular customers who had it at that time, they had to run it a lot of hours. They paid for fuel and for their operator. Sometimes, one of the Caterpillar engineers or even I went out to run it on weekends because they wanted lots of hours. Most of it was heavy tillage work, heavy chiselling. Big disks. We tried everything as much as possible.

"It was very exciting. And you know, we had a number of automobile wrecks that first year! People would be driving

1993 Challenger 70C

Right, the 70C was 12ft tall to the top of the stack, 19ft-4in long, and 10ft wide on 7ft-6in gauge. It weighed 36,200lb. Standard equipment included eight forward- and four rear-facing halogen lights.

1993 Challenger 70C

Upper far right, the side console contained the throttle control, transmission control, and implement hydraulics control levers. Hydraulic flow control valve knobs for implements set on circuit two or three were near the side window.

1993 Challenger 70C

Far right, wheelbase—track base— was 107in. These 35in wide belts— generating 4.8psi of ground pressure— incorporated four steel-belted plies. Longitudinal steel belts were one 3500ft continuous strand of 0.195in steel cable. These belts provided 4.8psi ground pressure.

1993 Challenger 70C

Bottom, the ten-speed Powershift transmission offered a top road speed of 18.1mph at 1900rpm. Shallow ripping in sandy soil such as this can be accomplished in fifth gear at nearly 6mph. The rubber tracks put nearly 8ft-10in of belt on the ground.

1993 Challenger 70C

Left, the near pedal was the service brake, the far one was clutch inching. Compartment heating and air conditioning as well as engine function gauges were on the front console. The automobile type steering wheel tilted 30 degrees and rotated only two full turns lock-to-lock.

1993 Challenger 70C

Far left, the 3306 inline six-cylinder diesel was turbocharged with an air-to-water intercooler. Its 4.75x6.00in bore and stroke yielded 638ci total displacement. Gross horsepower was rated at 285 at 2100rpm. Total fuel capacity was 210gal.

along, gazing off at this strange-looking tractor off in a field or going down the road. We had people run into each other.

"We had one of our customers driving by, saw it out in the field, and slowed down. He's looking out in the field, and the guy behind him was gawking out in the field, too. Only he didn't slow down. The guy rear-ended our customer! Then we started worrying about [whether] somebody was going to come back and sue us!

"One time, we moved it from one customer to another on the road. And two different sheriffs' departments and the Highway Patrol followed the machine. What was this thing going down the road? Was it legal? Nobody had seen a crawler tractor going down the road at 18mph. I had a number of them follow us, five, ten miles down the road. You could see these people talking on their radios. Pretty soon, another police car would show up, drive by the other way. It was funny.

"When we had the belted D3 a few years before, we were driving it over on the edge of the freeway over on Highway 99 at Route 70, heading back to the store in Sacramento. And a highway patrolman did pull us over. He got out of his car, looked at it, said, 'Oh, my gosh,' got back in his car, and drove off!"

But even while everyone enjoyed the crowd reactions, very little of the Challenger's testing and trials were fun and games. "It was like reinventing the wheel," McKeen contin-

ued. "Suspension was different, [the] steering system was different. That was the first time they came out with the direct-drive Powershift. They went to a bogey air suspension on the mid-rollers. Before that, they'd always had what's called a 'hard bottom.' Then when they came out with the High Drive tractors, they put on a kind of bogey system, but it was not mounted with an air ride suspension.

"I can remember during the test programs, things would show up and they were almost ready to throw up their hands and quit the whole project. Caterpillar had developed and tested a four-wheel-drive wheel tractor a couple years before. But they figured that was 'Me, too' and that they had to do something different. So they took that test bed machine, did a lot of conversions to it to try to make a rubber track out of that.

"By 1986—this is just before the scheduled introduction—they were experiencing different kinds of undercarriage problems. They broke some tracks early on, some came apart, the cables were not heavy enough. It was a certain kind of application that they had not experienced before: very wet, very sticky, and lots of build up."

Athorp knew about that problem. While it didn't happen on Boswell's ranch, news of it circulated widely. And Caterpillars' response made the grapevine as well. It made devoted customers as a result.

1995 Challenger RowCrop 55
Ground clearance was nearly 19in. The
maximum weight of the models was
25,000lb. These models used the same
differential steering motors of the older
Model 65s but the steering principle
was modified.

"Caterpillar was telling us, 'Hey, guys, we're going to build you a lightweight tractor with plenty of power,'" Athorp recalled, "'and we're going to give you the traction of a belt. Don't stack weight on this thing! If you do, you'll break it. You'll wind up shafts.'

"It didn't happen here. We didn't overload them. We had enough experience to know better. But hillside farming causes other problems. Friction drive. Slam on the brakes on a steep enough hill and you don't have enough friction. You don't stop. Belts would slip on the drive wheels. So the engineers went through a process of increasing the belt tensions.

"Now, understand, the original Challenger 65s were at 10,000lb belt tension. The engineers went at it in typical Caterpillar fashion. They decided to go to a 17,000lb tension. But Caterpillar just doesn't put a 17,000lb tensioner in and let it go. They understood that this increased all the load on the entire structure. They pulled final drives out. Resized the bearings. Did all the homework that Caterpillar always does.

All the Challengers came back to the yards. All the pieces [came] out, onto the scrap piles. [They] hired a guy to cut it up and haul it away. I heard—no one would ever confirm it—the in-house costs to Caterpillar were $30,000 per tractor to upgrade. And I can believe it because there was some big iron that came out. That," he said emphatically, "is the kind of product support you get out of those people."

For its efforts, Caterpillar was recognized by the American Society of Agricultural Engineers with its Concept of the Year Award in 1987 for the Challenger's mobil track system. With its sophisticated differential steering system, some early owner-operator customers likened it to driving their Cadillacs. McKeen knew first hand what it took to retain that kind of customer satisfaction.

"They spent a lot of money supporting that product," he explained. "I can look back at the first Challengers. I can remember some of the very first ones that we sold in December of 1986 and January of 1987, and I remember that Caterpillar spent more money on updates and conversions than they had sold the tractor for. But they had to face it! With a few test machines, you never get into every possible application and condition. It was a lot of hard learning, but they stuck with it. They hung in and brought out a very interesting machine. And now they can't build them fast enough!"

The next generation of Challengers are out in the fields, testing and proving themselves. Both Athorp and McKeen have had some time with Caterpillar's new Row Crop Challengers.

"We made our desires known," Athorp said coolly. "Low ground compaction. High horsepower-to-weight ratio. We wanted to have a variable-track gauge, just like a wheel tractor. We wanted it to do everything a wheel tractor would do with the advantages of a track-type machine.

"The farmers here want something like 5 1/2lb ground pressure, and it appears that with this new Row Crop Challenger, we are probably somewhere between 6lb and 9lb. We feel that we got somewhere around 25lb to 28lb with wheel tractors.

"One of the things that happens with this new Challenger is interesting. With the standard Challengers, the 65, 75, or 85, with the wide belts, or now with this new Row Crop 55, the tractor is no longer the controlling factor as to when we can get into the fields. The factor that controls how soon we can get into the fields is now the implement behind it. We can actually go across the ground with the Challenger, but the implement can't handle the wet conditions. It's a pretty dramatic change. It really gets into that sweet zone for ground prep and planting much better.

"When Caterpillar asked us about a row crop version of the Challenger, we encouraged them to build us a machine like that. Look, we appreciate the fact that while we are a large grower, we are not the whole act. The Midwest is a much larger consumer of this type of tractor than we are. Our goal is to be good cotton growers, not professional tractor developers or manufacturers. Up until fifteen years ago, we were just like everybody else, modifying a piece of existing equipment to do our job better. We took what was brought out by the makers and we worked to make it work for us.

"But now, this…." Athorp pointed to snapshot on his office wall. It was Caterpillar's Row Crop Challenger pulling a 50ft-wide chisel at work on the fields out behind his shops. "It's been a good relationship that has really opened up in the last fifteen years."

It's become a relationship that has put Caterpillar in an enviable position now. Its Row Crop Challengers offer a technologically advanced alternative for the four-wheel-drive markets in the Midwest.

"The Challenger changed some things for us and for our competition," McKeen said. "We started selling Challengers to customers who formerly had wheel tractors. Even here in California, customers who had gone to articulated wheel-type high-horsepower tractors are now using Challengers. And our competition has changed, too.

"Case bought out International Harvester, and they aren't building crawlers any more, really. Fiat bought Allis, and they're out. If you stop and look at it, the two biggest competitors in the Ag industry are John Deere and Case. I have a number of customers who never would buy a yellow tractor. Now, the orange and red don't make anything like what we have.

"This Row Caterpillar may push John Deere and Case into building rubber tracks. Where we are shooting at them right now is in their biggest volume for agricultural tractors. I've seen some pictures of rubber-track tractors from Deere and Case, and they have a lot of hard lessons to learn yet that Caterpillar has already been through. They're dealing with an outside supplier to make their tracks. And that's the other thing. To an outside supplier, a rubber track is just another product. But to Caterpillar, it's the whole machine."

Back in 1915, Philip Rose had spent as much time as he could talking with users as well as manufacturers of the tractors he investigated. After his examination of Best and Holt, he concluded that "small tractors will go slowly in the West. [I] met several farmers who own small, cheap tractors and use them for cultivating during the year, but contract their plowing and harvesting to men who have heavy machines for instance a 75-horsepower tractor will plow fifty

1995 Challenger RowCrop 55

As a row-crop tractor, the Challenger—available as a Model 35, 45, and 55 (shown here)—provided track gauge adjustable from 60–90in and track widths from 16–32in.

Starting Procedures for Caterpillar Challenger 75

1. Walk around the machine and inspect it for leaks or any other problem.
2. Check water and oil levels.
3. Get into the cab. Adjust the seat. Fasten the seatbelt. Adjust the steering wheel. Check and adjust the rearview mirror.
4. Turn the key and start the engine. Allow the engine to idle to warm up for at least 5 minutes, depending on the outside air temperature.
5. Monitor gauges and check for warning lights to make certain all engine functions are satisfactory.
6. Release the parking brake. Insert a cassette tape and adjust the volume on the tape cassette player.
7. Shift into gear and go.

---

acres of ground seven inches deep in a day. A 30 or 20hp will do only a quarter as much."

Athorp says his tractors must do 200 acres a day. And McKeen says that these days, Caterpillar spends as much time talking to its customers as it can. Several years after the first belted D3 and D6 started working the fields of California, Arizona, Oregon, and Washington, Caterpillar started sending not only its engineers but also its executives out to visit the operators to learn first hand how the products were being used.

"When the Challenger first came out," McKeen recalled, "a Caterpillar plane flew out here with three vice-presidents to watch the tractor work. We went out and saw the machine pull a laser-directed scraper and they all took a ride on it. And they were shocked! They couldn't believe that's what this machine was doing. That it was actually doing it. And then after that, they inaugurated some projects where some of the people on the assembly line came out—three or four people each trip—to visit some of the Challenger users to see what these machines that they had built were doing. There was a lot of spirit that came along from those plants with these people. And these visits were quite an eye-opener for everyone.

"I had two groups with me; each spent two days. We'd go around and visit people. And boy, one of the customers was a sour old guy. We were sitting around and this old guy was just running the Challenger down terribly to these people.

"Finally one of the factory people came over to me and said, 'Do you mind if I ask him why he bought it if he hated it so much?' [I answered,] 'Sure. Go ahead and ask him.' Right away, the guy broke a smile. He said, 'You're Caterpillar.' And he laughed and turned away. Now some of these people from the factory were feeling pretty bad. He had really been terrible to them. He turned back to them. 'Oh, it isn't as bad as I'm telling you. These problems we talked about, you're gonna cure them. You're gonna stay with it until it's finished and it's right.' He looked right at them and broke a broad grin. 'You're Caterpillar, and you don't back away from anything.'"

1995 Challenger RowCrop 55

Left, the Row Crop 35 and 45 used Caterpillar's Model 3116 engine, producing 175hp and 200hp. The Model 55 used a brand new inline six-cylinder 403ci diesel of 4.10x5.00in bore and stroke, producing around 225 gross horsepower. The turbocharger sat just above the hood latch.

1995 Challenger RowCrop 55

Below, pre-production prototypes deleted control markings because factory engineers introduced the machines to test operators. The difference between this prototype RowCrop side console and that of the new Challenger 70C reflected advances in ergonomics and user friendliness.

1995 Challenger RowCrop 55

Opposite page, weight-adjustable seats were carried over from production Challenger and steel-track models. Support and comfort controls made the operator's long days less taxing. The compartment was heated and air conditioned and offered a stereo casette player.

Index